Life After Death

Mysteries Revealed

Dr. Don T. Phillips

"Life After Death – Mysteries Revealed," by Don T. Phillips. ISBN 978-1-62137-932-4 (hardcover).

Published 2016 by Virtualbookworm.com Publishing Inc., P.O. Box 9949, College Station, TX 77845, US. ©2016 Don T. Phillips. All rights reserved. No part of this publication may be reproduced, stored in a retrieval system, or transmitted in any form or by any means, electronic, mechanical, recording or otherwise, without the prior written permission of Don T. Phillips.

Table of Contents

Chapter 1

The Nature of Man

Death is a part of every adult's life. The agony and pain experienced when a loved one dies is something that is experienced by almost everyone. Those who are alive and remain when a friend or family member passes on have a deep sense of loss and are faced with a puzzling question: *What next happens to a person who dies?* It is generally understood that there are 3 main states of existence which frame the answers to these and numerous other questions concerning *life after death.*

1.0 There is no life after death. Man is born into this world and will die in this world. After death, there is no longer any form of existence.

2.0 There is birth and death in this world, but not in the normal sense of conception or death. Each person or animal in existence possesses a soul, and that soul never dies. *Reincarnation* is the belief in a supreme being that watches over an endless cycle of creation, preservation, and dissolution. The soul is seen as eternal and part of a spiritual realm, and it will never cease to exist. Each soul returns to the physical realm in a new body. Reincarnation is not limited to being re-born as a human. Each soul might have had prior lives as animals, plants, or as divine beings who rule part of nature. If it has life, then it is part of the new cycle. A soul will complete this cycle of life many times, learning new things each time and working through its *karma.* This continuous cycle of existence is called *samsara.*

3.0 Man and all living creatures were created by an omniscient and omnipotent God. The cycle of life is started by natural childbirth, and ends in physical death. Man is composed of a body and a spirit. After death, the spiritual man transcends to a new plane of existence and is judged by God. The wicked are condemned to a spiritual death and cease to exist, and the pure in heart are granted eternal life. The criteria by which one qualifies for eternal life varies from one religion to another, but all support a spiritual afterlife or a spiritual death.

This book rejects the doctrines of both reincarnation and the total cessation of physical and spiritual life at death. It accepts the belief in only one God and one Son of God: Jesus Christ. Christianity is based upon the belief that there is only one eternal God who created the world and all of its inhabitants. His crowning creational achievement was Adam and Eve who were created pure and without sin. God gave Adam the *breath of life*, and he became a *living soul.*

And the LORD God formed man of the dust of the ground, and breathed into his nostrils the breath of life; and man became a living soul.   Genesis 2:7

Adam and Eve were told to have dominion over the earth that God had created, and to *replenish* the earth with their offspring (Genesis 1:26-28). Adam and Eve were placed into the Garden of Eden and were to live forever in communion with God. They were to be sustained by the Tree of Life that stood in the midst of Eden. However, both were deceived by Satan and sinned against God. No longer sinless, they were cast out of the Garden of Eden and began a new, mortal life. Since they had sinned against God and were banished from the Garden of Eden, they and all of their offspring were to experience death and possess the sin nature. The record of this tragic event and of how God dealt with mankind after the fall is contained in the Holy Bible. In His mercy, God created a plan by which all of mankind could be redeemed and brought back into a personal relationship with Him. That plan was to send His only begotten Son, Jesus Christ, to earth to save every person who would believe upon His Holy name. Jesus Christ conquered sin and Satan by living a sinless life, and then sacrificed Himself as the perfect Lamb of God on the cross of Calvary. By His sinless life and perfect sacrifice, He took upon Himself *all* of the sins of the world and offered eternal life to all who would believe upon His name; *He who knew no sin became sin for us* (II Corinthians 5:2). Christ rose from the grave, defeated death and Satan, and became the *firstfruit* harvest of all who would accept Him as their Lord and Savior. However, the penalty of physical death did not change. Man was born into sin, and everyone who ever lived or will live has sinned against God.

*Wherefore, as by one man sin entered into the world, and death by sin; and so death passed upon **all** men, for that **all** have sinned.*   Romans 5:12

When Jesus Christ died on the Cross of Calvary, the sins of every person who ever lived were permanently forgiven.

[14] *For by one offering he hath perfected for ever them that are sanctified.*
[15] *Whereof the Holy Ghost also is a witness to us: for after that he had said before,*
[16] *This is the covenant that I will make with them after those days, saith the Lord, I will put my laws into their hearts, and in their minds will I write them;*
[17] *And their sins and iniquities will I remember no more.*   Hebrews 10:14-17

The gift of eternal life is now offered to anyone who would have faith in Jesus Christ. Because Adam and Eve were cast out of the Garden of Eden, they began to die physically and every person that followed was condemned to physical death. We are still left with the following set of burning questions: *What happens to a person who dies? Does that person experience Joy? Pain? Remembrance? If that person continues to exist, in what form? Where? Will everyone that believes in Jesus Christ live forever? Will all of those who hear the gospel message and then reject Jesus Christ live forever? How? and where? Where do the dead currently exist?*

It is proposed that the answer to these and numerous other questions can be found in only one place: The *Holy Bible*. This book will address and answer those questions and others by seeking wisdom and truth from the one source of absolute wisdom and truth: *Jehovah God*, who has revealed both Himself and His Son to us in His Holy Bible.

[16] *All scripture is given by inspiration of God, and is profitable for doctrine, for reproof, for correction, for instruction in righteousness:*
[17] *That the man of God may be perfect, thoroughly furnished unto all good works.*
II Timothy 3:16-17

For any Christian who believes in biblical inerrancy, the Holy Scripture is the recorded *actual Words of God*, and carries the full authority of God. Every single statement of the Bible calls for instant and unqualified acceptance. Every doctrine of the Bible is the teaching of God and therefore requires full agreement. Every promise of the Bible calls for unshakable trust in its fulfillment. Every command of the Bible is a directive of God himself and therefore demands willing observance. Guided by the Holy Spirit for wisdom and understanding, we will seek and find the truth.

The Composition of Man

When God created Adam, He made him by reaching down into the dust of His earth and molding him into His own likeness (Genesis 1:26). Adam was now a perfect man with all of the organs and parts that sustain life, but he was lifeless. God then *breathed into his nostrils the breath of life; and man became a living soul* (Genesis 2:7). The lifeless Adam was quickened to mortal life by the very breath of God. It was with this act that life for all of mankind began. As part of this creative act, Adam *became a living soul*. Note that Adam was not changed into a different creature, but he became a living soul. He was fully man that possessed a soul given to him by God. We will later further discuss the eternal impact of this transformation in Chapter 2, but for now we will simply state that Adam lived because God breathed life into him, and then God gave Adam a soul to fully interact with the physical world. We will see that the *soul* of man is that component of man which links the smell, sight, hearing, taste and touch of man to that marvelous organ called the *brain*. We quote the following from Miles Grant:

> *Shall we dispute the Holy record and say that man was not formed out of dirt? Why believe the Lord? He said that man was made of dust from the ground! When modern science analyzed man it found that he is composed of carbon, oxygen, hydrogen, nitrogen, sulphur, phosphorus, iron and lime. These are earthly substances! When God created man from these raw materials He made the most wonderful mechanism known to exist. The lungs were prepared with millions of cells to capture oxygen, and then place oxygen in blood cells to sustain life; for life is in the blood. The heart pumps the blood through the body back to the lungs after being purified and filtered. The digestive system processes food to fuel our system, and the miraculous brain coordinates and controls every part of the body.*

It should be understood that *every* creature made by God also has the ability to live, breath, experience pain, etc. The difference between man and other living creatures is that man is composed of both *a physical* man and a true *spiritual man.* the spiritual component of man also comes from God, and it is that unique part of man that enables him to communicate with God. In the Garden of Eden, Adam and Eve had no need to receive the *spirit.* They were sustained by the Tree of Life which grew in the Garden of Eden and they walked and talked with God personally. As long as Adam and Eve obeyed God, they were allowed to live in perfect harmony with God and animals. The ancient Book of Enoch tells us that Adam and Eve actually talked with the animals. When Adam and Eve both sinned, all of these privileges vanished. God cannot coexist with sin because He is pure and Holy. When Adam and Eve were cast out of the Garden of Eden, they: (1) lost eternal life which was sustained by the Tree of Life, and (2) they no longer were able to walk with God because of sin. But, Adam and Eve were still God's creation and they needed to seek the forgiveness of sin by believing that God would send a redeemer who would take away sin(s). This belief in God and His ability to save them required a basic understanding of God and an ability to spiritually approach him. This was granted to man in the form of a *spirit* which would uniquely coexist with the *body* and *soul.* The body of man is mortal; the soul and spirit of man is immortal.

*...for the things which are **seen** are **temporal**; but the things which are **not seen** are eternal*
II Corinthians 4:18

You are not a *body with a soul.* You are a *soul with a body.* Your body will return to the dust of the ground. The Bible calls death putting off this tabernacle or dissolving this earthly house.

*For we know that if our **earthly** house of this tabernacle were dissolved, we have a building of God, an house not made with hands, **eternal** in the heavens.*   II Corinthians 5:1

For what is a man profited, if he shall gain the whole world, and lose his own soul?
Matthew 16:26

When man dies, the body returns to the dust from which it came and the spirit returns to God from which it came (Ecclesiastes 12:7); but the soul-man lives on (Daniel 12:2). The Christian who seeks to understand these *mysteries* should never confuse the spirit given to Adam and Eve with the Holy Spirit which was given by Christ to anyone who accepts him by *faith* as their long-awaited redeemer and savior. The acceptance of Jesus Christ as anyone's personal savior is *sealed* by being *born again,* and that sealing is *guaranteed* by the gift of the Holy Spirit. These truths will be fully discussed in Chapter 2.

The Destiny of Man

Adam and Eve were created in god's own image, and they were to *walk with God* (Genesis 3:8). They were sinless and were given access to the *Tree of Life* to nourish and keep them from aging. As long as they lived and communed with God in this sinless state, there was no need of being filled with the Spirit of God to serve as an intermediator between God and man. Their destiny was to live forever being sustained by the Tree of Life. When Adam and Eve sinned against God, they were alienated from His holy presence and were sent to live outside the

Garden. Man would now have to work and till the land by the sweat of his brow. The land was cursed by God, and thistles and thorns would be constantly attacking the fruit of the soil (Genesis 3:17-19). Because Eve believed Satan and tempted Adam, she was to feel pain and suffering in childbirth (Genesis 3:16). The most devastating result of sin was that Adam and Eve and all of their offspring were now sentenced to physical death without the nourishment of The Tree of Life. Adam lived for 930 years after he was banned from the Garden of Eden, but he eventually died as all of the offspring which would follow him (Genesis 5:5).

The question needs to be asked once again: *Was all man condemned to immediate and final death by sinning against God, or is man destined to live forever after his life on earth?* This question has been addressed many times by many different people. The answer is that if anyone today accepts Jesus Christ as their Lord and savior, the body of that person dies and returns to the dust from which it was formed (Job 34:15). *By the sweat of your face you shall eat bread, till you return to the ground, for out of it you were taken; for you are dust, and to dust you shall return* (Genesis 3:19). Mortal man must die a natural death, but life does not terminate at physical death. This issue should be forever settled by the words of John the Apostle.

*For God so loved the world, that he gave his only begotten Son, that whosoever believeth in him should not perish, **but have everlasting life.*** John 3:16

It is probably true that of all the verses contained in the Holy Bible, John 3:16 is perhaps the best known and the most often quoted. It contains the very essence of being a true Christian believer. Without any controversy or misunderstanding, John stated that anyone who believes in Jesus Christ will *inherit eternal life* (I John 2:17). Paul reveals to us that: *In whom also we have obtained an **inheritance**, being predestinated according to the purpose of him who worketh all things after the counsel of his own will* (Ephesians 1:11). Other passages that mention a believer's inheritance include Colossians 3:24 and Hebrews 9:15, and our reward is in heaven. In the world today, there are only two classes of people: those who believe that Jesus Christ died for our sins, and by faith in Him is offered eternal life; and those who do not believe in Jesus Christ. True believers who are born again will never die but will inherit the eternal kingdom *prepared for them before the foundation of the world* (Matthew 25:34). God is patient and *longsuffering* that none should perish. All unbelievers are destined for eternal punishment in the Lake of Burning Fire (Revelation 20:15). This will be discussed in more detail in Chapter 2.

*The Lord is not slack concerning his promise, as some men count slackness; but is **longsuffering** to us-ward, not willing that any should perish, but that all should come to repentance.* II Peter 3:9

We are assured that a place in the eternal Kingdom of God has been prepared for all born-again believers, and that their name has been written in the *Book of Life*. Christ told John to record the following promise to all believers.

*He that overcometh, the same shall be clothed in white raiment; and I will not blot out his name out of the **Book of Life**, but I will confess his name before my Father, and before his angels.*
Revelation 3:5

Later in the Book of Revelation, Christ is revealing that no one will be able to enter into the New Jerusalem unless their name is recorded in the *Lamb's Book of Life*. This is identical to the Book of Life He identified in Revelation 3:5.

*And there shall in no wise enter into it anything that defileth, neither whatsoever worketh abomination, or maketh a lie: but they which are written in the **Lamb's Book of Life.***
Revelation 21:27

We are also sure that there is no other way to inherit the promises made by Jesus Christ than to accept Him as their personal Lord and Savior. All *unbelievers* will be judged at the Great White Throne judgment following the 1000-year millennial kingdom, and those whose names are not found written in the Book of Life will be cast into the Burning Lake of Fire (Revelation 20:11-15). There is a theological controversy concerning whether or not the soul of an unbeliever will be consumed by fire and brimstone and cease to exist, or whether a nonbeliever will be tortured forever and be eternally separated from God. To a biblical literalist, there is really no controversy at all. Christ Himself told His disciples on the Mount of Olives that when He returns at His 2nd advent, that there will be a separation of sheep from goats.

[41] *Then shall he say also unto them on the left hand, Depart from me, ye cursed, into everlasting fire, prepared for the devil and his angels:*
[42] *For I was an hungred, and ye gave me no meat: I was thirsty, and ye gave me no drink:*
[43] *I was a stranger, and ye took me not in: naked, and ye clothed me not: sick, and in prison, and ye visited me not.*
[44] *Then shall they also answer him, saying, Lord, when saw we thee an hungred, or athirst, or a stranger, or naked, or sick, or in prison, and did not minister unto thee?*
[45] *Then shall he answer them, saying, Verily I say unto you, Inasmuch as ye did it not to one of the least of these, ye did it not to me.*
[46] *And **these shall go away into everlasting punishment**: but the righteous into life eternal.*
Matthew 25:41-46

The following verses written by the Apostle Timothy should settle this controversy once and for all. Either we believe what Jesus Christ told as recorded in the Holy scriptures or we do not.

[16] *All scripture is given by inspiration of God, and is profitable for doctrine, for reproof, for correction, for instruction in righteousness:*
[17] *That the man of God may be perfect, thoroughly furnished unto all good works.*
II Timothy 3:16-17

The Complete Man: Body, Soul and Spirit

God made Adam *in His own image*. We do not know what God looks like, but according to Genesis 1:26 we can assume that when we meet God in Heaven, He will resemble man in both form and appearance. When *Mary Magdalene* and the *other Mary* went to the tomb of Jesus Christ *early* on the *first day of the week* she found that Christ had risen from the grave and was not there. An angel appeared to the two women and commanded them to go and tell the disciples that Christ had risen from the grave. As both hurried along the road to find the disciples, Jesus Christ suddenly appeared to them in His resurrected body and greeted them. The women recognized His voice and then recognized Him, and they fell down and *held Him by the feet* (Matthew 28:1-10). Two things are obvious: (1) Christ had already ascended to the father and received his new, glorified body, and (2) The women recognized the risen Christ by both voice and appearance. This is proof that when those who accept Christ as their savior will still be recognized when they receive their new heavenly body. Later Christ appeared to all of the disciples and they recognized Him (Luke 24:39). This is not proof that God will resemble man in appearance, but since Jesus Christ is the Son of God we might assume that God is not a formless mass but similar to man (Genesis 1:26).

From the moment that a child is formed and lives in a mother's womb, a person exists as both a *physical* and a *spiritual* creature. The following two scriptures prove that every man and woman is composed of a physical body and two spiritual components: a *soul,* and a *spirit*.

And the very God of peace sanctify you wholly; and I pray God your whole spirit and soul and body be preserved blameless unto the coming of our Lord Jesus Christ.
          I Thessalonians 5:23

For the word of God is quick, and powerful, and sharper than any two edged sword, piercing even to the dividing asunder of soul and spirit, and of the joints and marrow, and is a discerner of the thoughts and intents of the heart.   Hebrews 4:12

The Body of Man

It is clear that the body is not unique to mankind; all living creatures have a body. But, the body of man is a marvelous act of creation. It is interesting that every man and woman is so unique that each can be distinguished from one another. The body is the interface of man to the outside world. It is this outer man that other people see. The body is mortal and will be returned to the dust from which it came at death. The *inner man* cannot be seen, and it consists of the *soul* and the *spirit*. Both the soul and the spirit live on after death, but the body is destroyed. The soul and the spirit are the two supernatural and spiritual aspects that Holy Scripture ascribes to humanity. It can be confusing to attempt to discern the precise difference between the two. Humans possess a spirit, but they are not spirits. Spirits can only be created by God and cannot die. At death, the spirit part of man separates from the soul and it returns to God from whence it came. We will see that the soul of a believer is transported to a place called *Paradise*, and the soul of an unbeliever is escorted to a place called *Torments* where they await the judgment of God. All true believers in Jesus Christ as the Son of God, who offers eternal life and salvation in the world to come, are said to be *spiritually alive* (1 Corinthians 2:11; Hebrews 4:12; James 2:26), while all unbelievers are said to be *spiritually dead* (Ephesians 2:1-5; Colossians 2:13). Humans were created and designed to have a personal relationship with God, and He created us with both *seen* and *unseen* parts. The part that is seen is obviously that which can be touched and recognized - the physical body (bones, organs, etc.), and the body functions as long as the person is alive. The unseen parts of a human are those which are hidden from the natural man: soul, spirit, intellect, conscience, etc.

The Spirit of Man

The *Spirit* of man is that inner component of man which gives any individual the ability to have an intimate relationship with God. Today when anyone is born again and by faith accepts Jesus Christ as their Lord and Savior, Jesus Christ sends the *Holy Spirit* to that person (Romans 8:9; 1 Corinthians 6:19-20, 12:13). Once a person is saved, they belong to Christ: They become a part of the Body of Christ and will be a part of His Bride in the afterlife. The Holy Spirit takes up residence in our hearts as long as we are alive, sealing us with the confirming, certifying, and assuring pledge of our salvation.

[16] *And I will pray the Father, and he shall give you another Comforter, that he may abide*
with you for ever;
[17] *Even the Spirit of truth; whom the world cannot receive, because it seeth him not, neither*
knoweth him: but ye know him; for he dwelleth with you, and shall be in you.
[18] *I will not leave you comfortless: I will come to you.*   John 14:6, 16-18

The Greek word translated *Comforter* in John 14:16 means *one who is called alongside* and has the idea of someone who encourages, exhorts and gives understanding. Jesus gave the Holy Spirit as a guarantee that He will return for all those who belong to Him. The gift of the Holy Spirit is also a *power gift*, and it enables a Christian to wage spiritual warfare against Satan.

[5] *For John truly baptized with water; but ye shall be baptized with the Holy Ghost not many*
days hence.
[8] *But ye shall receive power, after that the Holy Ghost is come upon you: and ye shall be*
witnesses unto me both in Jerusalem, and in all Judaea, and in Samaria, and unto the
uttermost part of the earth.   Acts 1:5-8

The Soul of Man

The *soul* of man is the battleground of the body, where Satan and man continually war with one another. The soul interacts with the physical man and the outside world through the five bodily senses of *sight, smell, hearing, taste* and *touch*. The reaction of man to the five senses which interact with the sin nature of man is dictated by the interaction of the soul with the spirit. The soul receives lust and immorality from the sinful outward man, and then determines the response desired by God through the help and power of discernment through the spirit man.

Dearly beloved, I beseech you as strangers and pilgrims, abstain from fleshly lusts, which war against the soul.   I Peter 2:11

The soul consists of the mind (which includes the conscience), the will and the emotions. The soul and the spirit are mysteriously tied together, and both are intimately linked to the body and mind. These are mysterious things which only God can explain. When God breathed His spirit into the lifeless body of Adam, Adam became a *living soul* The spirit of God supernaturally merged with the body and the soul.

The word *soul* in Hebrew is *nephesh*, meaning an animated, breathing, conscious, and living being. Man did not become a living soul until God breathed *nephesh* life into him. As a physical, animated, rational, and spiritual being, man is unique among all living things upon the earth.

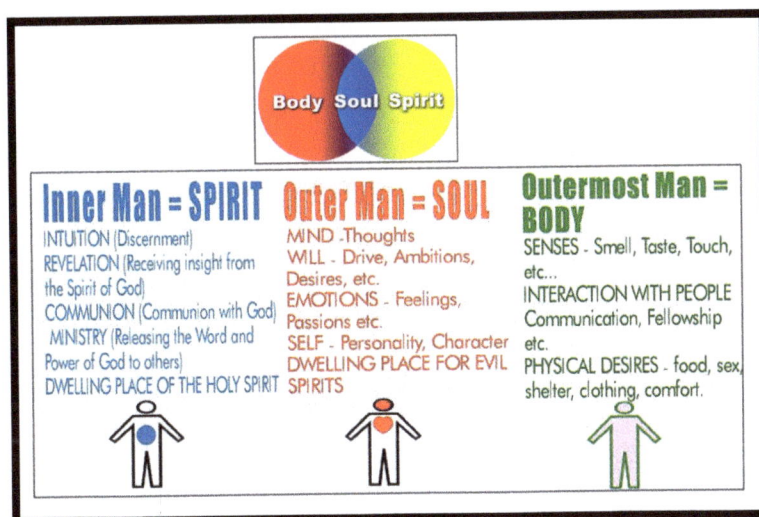

So, what is the *breath of God*? It is the life and power of God, given to man to bring him to life. The Hebrew word for *spirit* is *ruach*, which means wind, breath, air, spirit. The *life* given by God was designed to live eternally. The only question is *where will we live*? We will fully discuss these mysteries in subsequent chapters.

The soul is the component of man which will live forever, and it is what distinguishes mankind from every other living creature. We will now address a question that is important to any person who has ever had a pet: *Do animals have a soul*? The answer might surprise an average Christian: Yes, animals do have a soul. The soul is that component of man and animal that makes the body *divinely function*. The difference is in the eternal nature of the soul. The soul of man was created to live forever, but the soul of an animal will die when the animal dies. Recall that in

Genesis 2, God made Adam out of the dust of the earth; he was a perfect, created object with no life but he possessed all of the external and internal systems to function as a living creature. God then breathed the *breath of life* into Adam and he became a *living soul*. Adam could see, think, move and reason for himself. All of his mortal components - the brain, the heart, the lungs, the eyes, the ears, the organs, etc., began to function with one another. Adam was not a person with a soul, but he became a living soul.

[7] *And the LORD God formed man of the dust of the ground, and breathed into his nostrils the breath of life; and man became a living soul.*   Genesis 2:7

Modern science has determined that animals can think, reason and react to pain. It should be clear that without a soul, any animal, mammal or fowl would be as lifeless as Adam was when he was created. The soul is the very foundation of life. Animals are all living things; they have souls, but not in the sense in which human beings have souls. Animals can't do anything beyond the basic functions of mere existence. Although some animals are clever and possess a form of reasoning, they don't actually possess full conceptual intelligence. Animals and plants also lack a true moral sense. When you scold your pet dog for chewing the carpet and tell him what he did was wrong, the understanding is not conceptual but based upon the tone of your voice or in a limited sense the punishment which is given. Dogs cannot extract this experience to other related circumstances. Animals all live a temporal life, and they cease to exist at death. The soul of an animal does not live on after death, but in physical existence it was a soul. Human souls, by contrast, aren't material. They are spiritual. Sorry, but there is no *doggie heaven*. Finally, in some mysterious way that is not explained to us, heaven already has some animals that were created by God and are already living there. They must exist in some sort of spiritual/bodily form with the power to think, reason, etc. When Christ returns to take us to heaven with Him, He will be riding a white horse (Revelation 19:11).

Spirit	Soul	Body
God-breathed Breath of life	Consummation of body and spirit Living soul	Ground/dust Dust of the ground
God-conscious	Self-conscious	World-conscious
Man communicates with God, worships God serves Him and understands the relationship with God	Intellect which makes man's existence possible	5 organs / 5 senses Physical body to communicate to the physical world
God dwells in the spirit	Self dwells in the soul	Senses dwell in the body

Chapter 2

Abodes of the Dead

Death is something that every living person will experience, except when Christ returns at *the last trump* to resurrect the dead in Christ and to rapture out any living Christian before the *Wrath of God* falls upon the earth.

*For God hath not appointed us to **wrath**, but to obtain salvation by our Lord Jesus Christ.*   I
    Thessalonians 5:9

*And I heard a great voice out of the temple saying to the seven angels, Go your ways, and pour out the vials of **the wrath of God** upon the earth.*   Revelation 16:1

*For the **wrath of God** is revealed from heaven against all ungodliness and unrighteousness of men, who hold the truth in unrighteousness.*   Romans 1:18

[51] *Behold, I show you a mystery; We shall not all sleep, but we shall all be changed,*
[52] *In a moment, in the twinkling of an eye, at the last trump: for the trumpet shall sound, and the dead shall be raised incorruptible, and we shall be changed.*
[53] *For this corruptible must put on incorruption, and this mortal must put on immortality.*
[54] *So when this corruptible shall have put on incorruption, and this mortal shall have put on immortality, then shall be brought to pass the saying that is written, Death is swallowed up in victory.*   I Corinthians 15: 51-54

The apostle Paul provided a deeper understanding of this tremendous event in his letter to the church at Thessalonica.

[13] *But I would not have you to be ignorant, brethren, concerning them which are asleep, that ye sorrow not, even as others which have no hope.*
[14] *For if we believe that Jesus died and rose again, even so them also which sleep in Jesus will   God bring with him.*
[15] *For this we say unto you by the word of the Lord, that we which are alive and remain unto the coming of the Lord shall not prevent them which are asleep.*
[16] *For the Lord himself shall descend from heaven with a shout, with the voice of the archangel, and with the trump of God: and the dead in Christ shall rise first:*
[17] *Then we which are alive and remain shall be caught up together with them in the clouds, to meet the Lord in the air: and so shall we ever be with the Lord.*
[18] *Wherefore comfort one another with these words.*   I Thessalonians 4:13-18

Death is an event which is feared and seriously misunderstood by every person whether they are saved or unsaved. *What happens to a person when life leaves the body? Is death simply passing from one plane of existence to another? Where does the soul of a person go when it departs the body? Does the soul of a person live forever? Is death a different experience for believers from unbelievers?* We will now address these and other important questions.

Where does the soul of a person go when it departs the body?

When Adam and Eve sinned, they were cast out of the Garden of Eden and both began to physically die. When they were removed from Eden, time began as we know it today. The sun and the rotation of the earth around the sun make a solar day equivalent to 24 hours (approximately). The amount of time it takes the earth to orbit the sun is 365 days, 5 hours, 48 minutes and 46 seconds, and this is one year. Adam lived to be 930 years old (Phillips, *A Chronology of Man*), and about 4,000 years passed between when recorded time began and Christ was crucified. It has also been shown that the Dispensation of the Law ended and the Dispensation of Grace began on the same day; Wednesday, April 5, 30 AD; which is the day that Christ was crucified (Phillips *The Birth and Death of Jesus Christ*).

As discussed in Chapter 1, Man is composed of two parts: (1) A *physical* man, and (2) A *spiritual* man. The physical man is the external shell called the *body*. The spiritual man is composed of the *spirit* and the *soul*. The body was made by God from the dust of the earth, and to dust it will return. When a person dies, the *spirit* will separate from the body and return to God, from which it came.

*All flesh shall perish together, and man shall turn again unto **dust.*** Job 34:15

Then shall the dust return to the earth as it was: and the spirit shall return unto God who gave it. Ecclesiastes 12:7

At death, the *soul* will be transported to a place called *Hades or Sheol*. Sheol is composed of two separate compartments: one called *Paradise,* and the other a *Place of Torments*. At death, the soul of a born-again believer is transported to Paradise; the soul of an unbeliever is transported to the Place of Torments (Luke 16).

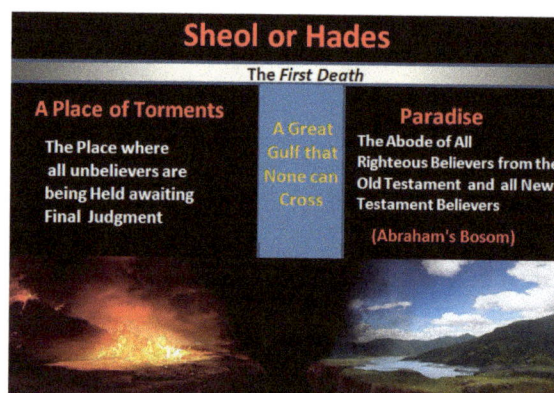

Sheol or Hades

The *First Death*

A Place of Torments

The Place where all unbelievers are being Held awaiting Final Judgment

A Great Gulf that None can Cross

Paradise

The Abode of All Righteous Believers from the Old Testament and all New Testament Believers

(Abraham's Bosom)

Sheol is the Old Testament translation of the Hebrew word *She'ole'*. When the Hebrew Old Testament scriptures were translated into Greek in ancient Alexandria around 200BC, the word *Hades* (the Greek underworld) or Hell was substituted for Sheol. The first mention of the word hell in the Holy Bible is found in Deuteronomy.

*For a fire is kindled in mine anger, and shall burn unto the lowest **hell**, and shall consume the earth with her increase, and set on fire the foundations of the mountains.*

Deuteronomy 32:22

The Hebrew word translated *hell* in this verse is *Sheol*. The first use of the word hell in the New Testament is found in the Book of Matthew.

*But I say unto you, That whosoever is angry with his brother without a cause shall be in danger of the judgment: and whosoever shall say to his brother, Raca, shall be in danger of the council: but whosoever shall say, Thou fool, shall be in danger of **hell** fire.*

Matthew 5:22

The Greek word translated *hell* in this passage is *Gehenna*. Gehenna is not Sheol, but it is a subterranean compartment which is also called the Lake of Burning Fire. We will discuss Gehenna in some detail later, but for now understand that the word hell in the Holy Scriptures is used to (improperly) represent many Hebrew or Greek places.

The Authorized King James version of the Bible uses the word *hell* 64 times throughout the Old and New Testaments. Unfortunately, the translated word *hell* does not always come from Sheol or Gehenna, but also from *Tartarus*. Both Tartarus and Gehenna are Greek words for underworld dungeons which we will discuss later. *Sheol* is found in the Bible sixty-five times. It is poorly translated as the *pit* three times, the *grave* thirty-one times, and *hell* thirty-one times. The Greek word *Hades* is used eleven times, being translated *hell* ten times and the *grave* once. Adding to the confusion is that two other Greek words were also translated as hell in the KJV New Testament. These are *Tartarus*, which is found once, and *Gehenna* which is used twelve times. Because of poorly translated verses from Greek to English, the place called hell is commonly misunderstood to mean a place of torment where the souls of the wicked go after physical death. The truth of the matter is that there is *not one single word* in the Hebrew and Greek Manuscripts of the Bible that in its root form means hell. Any place commonly translated as hell visualizes a place of fire and anguish. Hell is a man-invented, pagan, unchristian, heretical belief that was first embraced and Christianized by Roman Catholicism, and incorporated into the Bible by Jerome through his Latin Vulgate in the early history of Christianity. Psalm 89:48 speaks of death of being that instant in which the soul separates from the body. The body is given over to the grave where it will decay, while the soul is assigned to either Paradise or the Place of Torments which are contained in Sheol/Hades to await the final judgment. We will later see that Gehenna and Tartarus are both real compartments which exist in the lowest parts of the earth.

Tartarus is where those angels who co-habitated with women before the flood are being held for final judgment. (II Peter 2:4). Gehenna is a place where the souls of those who have refused to accept Jesus Christ will be sent after they are judged at the Great White Throne Judgment (Revelation 20:14-15). Gehenna is believed to be the final destination of all unbelievers, and is a Great Lake of Burning Fire. It is also called the *abyss*.

Sheol or Hades

Hades or Sheol is composed of two compartments: (1) *Paradise,* and (2) *A Place of Torments* (Luke 19:16-26*).* In both the Old and New Testaments, the souls of those who die in faith were taken to a place called *Paradise* and the souls of all those who died without faith were taken to a place called *Torments*. In the Gospel of Luke, the story of the rich man and Lazarus (Luke 16:19-31) speak of these two compartments, but the term *Abraham's Bosom* is used to describe Paradise. This is the only time that this term is used in the Holy Scriptures. The answer to the question of which compartment receives the soul is totally determined under the *New Covenant* by whether or not the person has accepted Jesus Christ as their redeemer and savior. If a person is born-again, that person's name will be recorded in

Sheol or Hades	
A Place of Torments	**Paradise**
The Place where all unbelievers are being Held awaiting Final Judgment	The Abode of All Righteous Believers from the Old Testament and all New Testament Believers

the *Lamb's Book of Life.* Every person who has their name written in either the Book of Life (Old Testament and New Testament) or in the Lambs Book of Life (New Covenant believers) will be given a new incorruptible, undefiled body by Jesus Christ at the *last trump*. Everyone who's name is in the Lamb's Book of Life will also have their name recorded in God's Book of Life but not vice-versa.

The *soul* of any New Covenant Christian who has had their name written in the Lamb's Book of Life will rest in the place called Paradise, where they will await the *Bema Seat Judgment* (Phillips, Revelation: *Mysteries Revealed*). The souls of those Old Testament believers who died possessing faith that a promised redeemer would arise who would take away their sins, either before or after the Law was given to Moses by God at Mt. Sinai, were also transported to the place called Paradise. Of course, the Old Testament saints had no way of knowing that their promised redeemer would be called Jesus Christ, but those who died in the faith of Abraham believed that they would live on after physical death in a special spiritual realm called *Sheol* in the Hebrew scriptures and *Hades* in the English translation (KJV) of the Greek manuscripts. This is made certain by the prayer that King David prayed to God before his death in the Old Testament and by the words of Christ as he addressed Peter and the rest of His disciples.

*For thou wilt not leave my soul in **hell**; neither wilt thou suffer thine Holy One to see corruption.*
Psalms 16:10

Hell in Psalms 16:10 is translated from the Hebrew word *She'ole'* or *sheol*.

Christ referred to a place called *Hades* when he blessed Peter because he responded in faith that Christ was surely the Son Of God.

*And I say also unto thee, That thou art Peter, and upon this rock I will build my church; and the gates of **hell** shall not prevail against i.t*   Matthew 16:18

The word *hell* in Matthew 16:18 is translated from the Greek word *Hades*.

The Jewish historian Josephus wrote of what happens to a person after death in his *Discourse to the Jews* (The original discourse is attributed to the church father, *Hippolytus* of Rome

> NOW as to **Hades**, wherein the souls of the of the good things they see, and rejoice in the righteous and unrighteous are detained, it is necessary to speak of it. Hades is a place in the world not regularly finished; **a subterraneous region**, wherein the light of this world does not shine; from which circumstance, that in this region the light does not shine, it cannot be but there must be in it perpetual darkness. This region is allotted as a place of custody for souls, in which angels are appointed as guardians to them, who distribute to them temporary punishments, agreeable to every one's behavior and manners. In this region there is a certain place set apart, as a lake of unquenchable fire, whereunto we suppose no one hath hitherto been cast; but it is prepared for a day afore-determined by God, in which one righteous sentence shall deservedly be passed upon all men; when the unjust, and those that have been disobedient to God, and have given honor to such idols as have been the vain operations of the hands of men, as to God himself, shall be adjudged to this everlasting punishment, as having been the causes of defilement; while the just shall obtain an incorruptible and never-fading kingdom. These are now indeed confined in Hades, but not in the same place wherein the unjust are confined. For there is one descent into this region, at whose **gate** we believe there stands an archangel with an host; which gate when those pass through that are conducted down by the angels appointed over souls, they do not go the same way; but the **just are guided to the right hand**, and are led with hymns, sung by the angels appointed over that place, unto a region of light, in which the just have dwelt from the beginning of the world; not constrained by necessity, but ever enjoying the prospect of the good things they see, and rejoice in the expectation of those new enjoyments which will be peculiar to every one of them, and esteeming those things beyond what we have here; with whom there is no place of toil, no burning heat, no piercing cold, nor are any briers there; but the countenance of the fathers and of the just, which they see always, smiles upon them, while they wait for that rest and eternal new life in heaven, which is to succeed this region. **This place we call The Bosom of Abraham**.

*But as to the **unjust, they are dragged by force to the left hand** by the angels allotted for punishment, no longer going with a good will, but as prisoners driven by violence; to whom are sent the angels appointed over them to reproach them and threaten them with their terrible looks, and to thrust them still downwards. Now those angels that are set over these souls, drag them into the neighborhood of hell itself; who, when they are hard by it, continually hear the noise of it, and do not stand clear of the hot vapor itself; but when they have a near view of this spectacle, as of a terrible and exceeding great prospect of fire, they are struck with a fearful expectation of a future judgment, and in effect punished thereby: and not only so, but where they see the place [or choir] of the fathers and of the just, even hereby are they punished; for a chaos deep and large is fixed between them; insomuch that a just man that hath compassion upon them cannot be admitted, nor can one that is unjust, if he were bold enough to attempt it, pass over it. This is the discourse concerning Hades, wherein **the souls of all men** are confined until a proper season, which God hath determined, when he will make a resurrection of all men from the dead, not procuring a transmigration of souls from one body to another, but raising again those very bodies, which you Greeks, seeing to be dissolved, do not believe [their resurrection]. But learn not to disbelieve it; for while you believe that the soul is created, and yet is made immortal by God, according to the doctrine of Plato, and this in time, be not incredulous; but believe that God is able, when he hath raised to life that body which was made as a compound of the same elements, to make it immortal; for it must never be said of God, that he is able to do some things, and unable to do others. We have therefore believed that the body will be raised again; for although it be dissolved, it is not perished; for the earth receives its remains, and preserves them; and while they are like seed, and are mixed among the more fruitful soil, they flourish, and what is sown is indeed sown bare grain, but at the mighty sound of God the Creator, it will sprout up, and be raised in a clothed and glorious condition, though not before it has been dissolved, and mixed [with the earth]. So that we have not rashly believed the resurrection of the body; for although it be dissolved for a time on account of the original transgression, it exists still, and is cast into the earth as into a potter's furnace, in order to be formed again, not in order to rise again such as it was before, but in a state of purity, and so as never to be destroyed any more. And to every body shall its own soul be restored. And when it hath clothed itself with that body, it will not be subject to misery, but, being itself pure, it will continue with its pure body, and rejoice with it, with which it having walked righteously now in this world, and never having had it as a snare, it will receive it again with great gladness. But as for the unjust, they will receive their bodies not changed, not freed from diseases or distempers, nor made glorious, but with the same diseases wherein they died; and such as they were in their unbelief, the same shall they be when they shall be faithfully judged. For all men, the just as well as the unjust, shall be brought before God the word: for to him hath the Father committed all judgment: and he, in order to fulfill the will of his Father, shall come as Judge, whom we call Christ.*

It is not a coincidence that the night before Jesus Christ was crucified, He spoke to His disciples concerning a future judgment called the *Judgment of the Sheep and Goats* (Matthew 25). We will discuss this later in Chapter 6, but for now we note that the people called His *sheep* were redeemed and sent to his *right hand*, and those who were condemned were called *goats* and were sent to His *left* hand. This corresponds to the separation spoken of by Josephus. My own research in the Holy Scriptures has confirmed the basic truth of a similar discourse by Hippolytus of Rome, and later quoted by Josephus with only a few exceptions. As previously discussed, upon death the soul of any New Testament believer who has had his name written in the *Lamb's Book of Life* is transported to the part of Sheol called *Paradise* where that person will reside in happiness until they will be given a new glorified body at the resurrection of all the righteous dead. Those whose names were not found in the Book of Life will be incarcerated in a place called *Torments*, where they will await their final sentencing at the *Great White Throne Judgment*. Their ultimate fate is to be cast into *Gehenna* or the *Lake of Burning Fire*. Gehenna will be discussed in some detail in Chapter 3.

Our New Resurrected Body

The soul is where the very essence of a living man or woman resides. It is where the physical body interacts with the spirit of man while a person is alive on this earth. At death, it will be transported to Paradise where it will remain until Christ will suddenly appear in the air and unite the soul with a new celestial body at the rapture. We do not know very much about that new body, but we do know that it will not be fueled by blood and it will not be covered with flesh as we now know it.

*Now this I say, brethren, that **flesh** and **blood** cannot inherit the kingdom of God; neither doth corruption inherit incorruption* I Corinthians 15:50

The resurrected body will be a spiritual framework which will house our soul. The natural body is remarkably created and configured for living in this world, but this is the only realm in which it will function. After the resurrection we will have a new incorruptible *spiritual body*, perfectly suited for not only living on this earth but also living in heaven. This does not mean that we will be *only* spirits because spirits do not have bodies. Our resurrected body will not need physical sustenance or depend on the natural means of supporting life.

[35] *But some man will say, How are the dead raised up? and with what body do they come?*
[36] *Thou fool, that which thou sowest is not quickened, except it die:*
[37] *And that which thou sowest, thou sowest not that body that shall be, but bare grain, it may chance of wheat, or of some other grain:*
[38] *But God giveth it a body as it hath pleased him, and to every seed his own body.*
[39] *All flesh is not the same flesh: but there is one kind of flesh of men, another flesh of beasts, another of fishes, and another of birds.*
[40] *There are also celestial bodies, and bodies terrestrial: but the glory of the celestial is one,*

and the glory of the terrestrial is another.

[41] There is one glory of the sun, and another glory of the moon, and another glory of the stars: for one star differeth from another star in glory.

[42] So also is the resurrection of the dead. It is sown in corruption; it is raised in incorruption:

[43] It is sown in dishonour; it is raised in glory: it is sown in weakness; it is raised in power:

[44] It is sown a natural body; it is raised a spiritual body. There is a natural body, and there is a spiritual body.　　　I Corinthians 15: 35-44

How the soul is joined to a new body from heaven is a *mystery* known only to God. We only know that the original body will in some mysterious way rise from its grave and be reunited with the soul in a new glorious form called our *heavenly body*.

Most Christians are aware that their soul will live forever within a new, undefiled, incorruptible body awarded to us by God. This is a basic belief under the *New Covenant* and has been guaranteed to all born-again believers by the resurrection of Jesus Christ after He spent 3 days and 3 nights in the grave. The *Holy Spirit* has been given to all New Covenant believers as a *guarantee* of His promise. However, this is such an important concept that it demands to be further discussed and justified later in this chapter; for now, consider the following relevant question.

Will Old Testament men and women, including the Jews, obtain salvation and eternal life since they all died in sin?

Both New Covenant saints and Old Testament saints are saved in the same way, *by faith*. The scriptures are quite clear that both groups of people can only obtain salvation by believing in faith that a redeemer would arise that would take away the sins of the entire world. All the Old Testament saints died in sin, but by faith they believed that someday God would send a redeemer who would take away their sins, never to be remembered, and that this redeemer would reward their faith with eternal life. Just as under the New Covenant, salvation to all Old Testament saints is offered by grace and not by works. Every New Testament saint is saved by believing that God sent that redeemer, and that He was Jesus Christ the Son of God. Jesus Christ died for the sins of the entire world, and He offers salvation and eternal life through His sacrificial death. Every Old Testament Jew and men of faith before them was saved by faith and grace, just as every New Testament believer is saved by faith and grace. The difference is that every Old Testament believer looked *forward* through time to the cross and every New Testament believer looks *backward* to the cross.

Another key difference is that the redeemer promised to all Old Testament saints was predicted and prophesied without knowing His *name*, but the *person* of Jesus Christ and His predestined appearance on earth should have been well-known and understood by all Old Testament believers. The Old Testament has well over 100 different scriptural references to Jesus Christ, including where He was to be born, the purpose of His ministry on earth, and that He would suffer and die a horrible death to redeem their sins. There is really no reason why any Old Testament believer would ever doubt that their promised redeemer would arise in the *fullness of time*. New Testament Saints have the work of Chris, His signs and miracles recorded in the four gospels (Matthew, Mark, Luke and John), and the epistles of Paul and other apostles. However, the actual personage of Jesus Christ was only seen over a short period of time. He died at 33.5 years of age after a 3.5-year ministry. Even during that time period, Jews and Gentiles that walked the earth with Christ were all saved by faith. Christ spent His entire earthly ministry proclaiming the *good news* that He was the Son of God sent to take away the sins of the world and that salvation would be offered by faith and grace. The Pharisees, Sadducees and the Jewish Priesthood all rejected His claims and failed to accept Him by faith. It was this same lack of faith and discernment that finally led them to crucify Jesus Christ on the cross of Calvary.

Jesus Christ the Son of God said:

*Jesus saith unto him, I am the **way**, the truth, and the life: no man cometh unto the Father, but by me.* John 14:6

*I am the **door**: by me if any man enter in, he shall be saved, and shall go in and out, and find pasture.* John 10:9

*He that believeth on me, as the scripture hath said, out of his belly shall flow rivers of **living** water.* John 7:38

*And whosoever liveth and believeth in me shall **never** die. Believest thou this?* John 11:26

In his letter to the Romans, the apostle Paul confirmed that salvation is obtained by faith and nothing else.

*For therein is the righteousness of God revealed from **faith** to **faith**: as it is written, The just shall live by **faith**.* Romans 1:17

[27] *Where is boasting then? It is excluded. By what law? of works? Nay: but by the law of **faith**.*
[28] *Therefore we conclude that a man is justified by **faith** without the deeds of the law.*
[30] *Seeing it is one God, which shall justify the circumcision by faith, and uncircumcision through faith.* Romans 3:27-30

The Soul after Death

Every person that ever lived before and after Jesus Christ died on the cross of Calvary committed sin: *For all have sinned, and come short of the glory of God* (Romans 3:23). Old Testament men and women died without their sins forgiven, because their long-awaited Messiah who would take away and forgive their sins had not yet appeared. So *what happened to these people at death?* In the Hebrew Scriptures, the word used to describe the realm of the dead is called *Sheol*. It means the *place of the dead* or the *place of departed souls*. The Greek New Testament equivalent to Sheol is *Hades*. Sheol is sometimes translated in English as *Hell*, and hell is usually associated with a place of torments. This is unfortunate, because Sheol or Hades refers to a place where the soul of every man, saved or unsaved, dwells after death. The word *Hell* never appears in the original Hebrew or Greek biblical manuscripts.

For thou wilt not leave my soul in hell; neither wilt thou suffer thine Holy One to see corruption.
Psalms 16:10

(The word *hell* is translated from the Hebrew word *sheol*)

We have previously shown that Sheol or Hades and was divided into two compartments: a place called *Paradise,* and a place called *Torments.* When an Old Testament person died in faith like Abraham (Hebrews 11), their soul was immediately taken to Paradise. The soul of an unbeliever was taken to a place called *torments.* The souls residing in Paradise were there by faith in the coming, promised Messiah who would take away their sins. The souls residing in the place of torments had died as unbelievers and await their final judgment and sentencing at the *Great White Throne Judgment* following the 1,000-year millennial kingdom.

Jacob said: For I will go down into the grave (Sheol) unto my son mourning.   Genesis 37:35

The Apostle Paul said:

[22] *And it came to pass, that the beggar died, and was carried by the angels into **Abraham's bosom**: the rich man also died, and was buried;*
[23] *And in **hell** (Hades) he lift up his eyes, being in torments, and seeth Abraham afar off, and Lazarus in his bosom.*   Luke 16:22-23

As Jesus Christ hung on the cross of Calvary, two thieves condemned to death who hung on His right and left. One mocked Jesus and the other asked Jesus to remember him when the Christ came into His kingdom. This simple act of faith was recognized by Jesus even in his time of anguish, and He replied:

And Jesus said unto him, Verily I say unto thee, Today shalt thou be with me in Paradise.
Luke 23:43

This is proof that when the repentant sinner died, his soul did not go straight to heaven, but to Paradise. We confirm this truth every time we recite the *Apostles Creed* that Christ descended into Sheole/Hades upon His death. What is meant by Paul saying that Christ descended into the *lower parts of the earth* upon His death for three days and three nights? His words in the original Greek manuscript was that He descended into descended into *Sheol/Hades*.

> *I believe in God, the Father Almighty, Creator of Heaven and earth;*
> *and in Jesus Christ, His only Son Our Lord, Who was conceived by the Holy Spirit, born of the Virgin Mary, suffered under Pontius Pilate, was crucified, died, and was buried. **He descended into Hell**; the third day He rose again from the dead;*
> *He **ascended** into Heaven, and sitteth at the right hand of God, the Father almighty; from thence He shall come to judge the living and the dead.*

The word *Hell* actually means Hades or Sheol as we have previously discussed. The Apostles Creed appeared for the first time in a letter, probably written in about 390AD by Ambrose, from a Council in Milan to Pope Siricius. The Roman Catholic Church kept and preserved this belief from that time forward as a sacred confirmation of faith. It was no doubt partly based upon a statement recorded by the Apostle Paul in his letter to the Ephesians.

[9] *Now that he ascended, what is it but that he also **descended** first into the lower parts of the earth?*
[10] *He that **descended** is the same also that ascended up far above all heavens, that he might fill all things.* Ephesians 4:9-10

Paul revealed that Christ did visit Hades during the 3 days and 3 nights His body lay in the grave, and He preached to the righteous souls who were being held in the compartment called *Paradise*. Christ had no reason to visit the unrighteous in a place called Torments. If anyone might believe that Hell/Hades is in fact a single place of *torments*, why would Christ descend into its depths? What purpose would it serve? Christ descended into the *compartment* of Hades/Sheol called *Paradise* to tell the Old Testament saints who had died in faith that He was their long-awaited Messiah. Luke confirmed this in his gospel when he recorded the very words of Christ.

*The Spirit of the Lord is upon me, because he hath anointed me to preach the gospel to the poor; he hath sent me to heal the brokenhearted, to **preach deliverance to the captives**, and recovering of sight to the blind, to set at liberty them that are bruised.* Luke 4:18

In his great sermon delivered on the Day of Pentecost in Jerusalem, Peter is assuring the Jews that were all gathered there that the soul of their great patriarch David was escorted to *Hades* upon his death, to Abraham's Bosom or Paradise.

.... thou wilt not leave my soul in hell (Hades), neither wilt thou suffer thine Holy One to see corruption. Acts 2:27

It should be noted Peter is quoting David from Psalms 16:10. In both Acts 2:27 and in Psalms 16:10 the phrase *Holy One* is capitalized. In the KJV this is always used when referring to God.

But it is clear that David is talking about *Jesus Christ*, God in the 2nd person of the Trinity. King David likely did not know that Jesus Christ was his redeemer, but he obviously knew that there would be one who would be sent by God in His name, and that this long-awaited Messiah would also visit Hades where he would be waiting. He was also sure that the Holy One he would long await would not allow his soul to experience any form of corruption. Peter went on to say that the patriarch, King David, was still in Paradise awaiting His resurrected body.

*Men and brethren, let me freely speak unto you of the patriarch **David**, that he is both dead and buried, and his sepulchre is with us unto this day.*   Acts 2:29

The soul of Christ descended into Hades, but He was there for only three days and three nights. Peter continues in his sermon to reveal that David and the term Holy One was indeed speaking of Jesus Christ the Son of God.

*He (David) seeing this before, spoke of the resurrection of Christ, that His soul was not left in **hell**, neither his flesh did see corruption.*   Acts 2:31

The New Testament Greek word for the Old Testament Hebrew word Sheol is Hades, and it is here translated as hell.

The Lord's body was placed into the tomb of Joseph (Matthew 27:59-60), but His *soul* went to Sheol/Hades. In both Acts 2:27 and Acts 2:31, the translators of the Greek New Testament should have used the Greek word *Hades* instead of *hell*. Our Lord Jesus Christ descended into Hades (Greek) or Sheol (Hebrew), which are both translated as hell in the English authorized KJV.

Acts 2:31 is strong confirmation that King David, by divine revelation, understood that he would go to a place called Hades/Sheol at death and remain there until Christ would resurrect him from the grave. Christ's soul was in Sheol/Hades between His death and resurrection, and the place where Christ's soul went between His death and resurrection was *Paradise* (Luke 23:43). After Christ preached the gospel message and good news for three days and three nights to those believers who had waited so long, He was resurrected and ascended to the Father. Christ was the firstfruit of all New Testament and Old Testament believers who would later follow Him out of Paradise at the *last trump*. Perhaps the most convincing narrative in the entire body of scripture that there are two compartments which hold the dead can be found in Luke 16:20-23 This proves that there are two compartments put in place by God to hold the souls of unbelievers and believers.

[20] *And there was a certain beggar named Lazarus, which was laid at his gate, full of sores,*
[21] *And desiring to be fed with the crumbs which fell from the rich man's table: moreover the dogs came and licked his sores.*
[22] *And it came to pass, that the beggar died, and was carried by the angels into Abraham's*

bosom: the rich man also died, and was buried;

[23] *And in hell he lift up his eyes, being in torments, and seeth Abraham afar off, and Lazarus in his bosom.*

[24] *And he cried and said, Father Abraham, have mercy on me, and send Lazarus, that he may dip the tip of his finger in water, and cool my tongue; for I am tormented in this flame.*

[25] *But Abraham said, Son, remember that thou in thy lifetime receivedst thy good things, and likewise Lazarus evil things: but now he is comforted, and thou art tormented.*

[26] *And beside all this, between us and you there is a great gulf fixed: so that they which would pass from hence to you cannot; neither can they pass to us, that would come from thence.*
Luke 16:20-26

Lazarus's place of comfort is called *Abraham's Bosom* and it is identical to *Paradise* (Luke 23:43). Between the two abodes of the dead there was *a great chasm* (Luke 16:26). The fact that no one could cross this chasm indicates that after death one's fate is sealed. Note that three days after Jesus told the *repentant thief* that he would be in Paradise with Him, He told Mary Magdalene, who first saw Him in resurrected form; *Do not cling to me, for I have not yet **ascended** to the My Father* (John 20:17). *When did Christ ascend to the Father?* He did not ascend until after 3 days and 3 nights in Hades, and clearly after the appearance to Mary Magalene. The sequence of events was clearly described by the Apostle Paul.

[8] *Wherefore he saith, When he **ascended** up on high, he led captivity captive, and gave gifts unto men.*

[9] *(Now that he ascended, what is it but that he also **descended first** into the lower parts of the earth?*

[10] *He that descended is the same also that ascended up far above all heavens, that he might fill all things.)*   Ephesians 4:8-10

Christ first *descended* to Paradise in the lower parts of the earth, He then *ascended* to His Father with *captives. Who were these captives?* It could not be the unbelievers in the Place of Torments, so it had to be the believers who were waiting in Paradise!

The Apostle Paul was allowed to visit and see Paradise while He was alive. He referred to himself as simply *a man*.

[2] *I knew a man in Christ above fourteen years ago, (whether in the body, I cannot tell; or whether out of the body, I cannot tell: God knoweth;) such an one caught up to the third heaven.*

[3] *And I knew such a man, (whether in the body, or out of the body, I cannot tell: God knoweth;)*

[4] *How that he was caught up into paradise, and heard unspeakable words, which it is not lawful for a man to utter*   II Corinthians 12:2–4

Comparing Luke 16:20-26 to Ephesians 4:8-10 and both to I Corinthians 12:2-4, it appears that after Christ visited Paradise to tell the Old Testament believers that He was their long awaited Messiah He emptied Paradise of all Old Testament saints (He led captivity captive) and moved them to a place in the 3rd heaven near the throne of God to await their final judgment; not for salvation but for rewards. Evidently Paradise was *moved* from the depths of the earth to the presence of God. This is thought to be true since Paul recorded that he had *ascended* into the third heaven and saw Paradise there. These are all conclusions that could only be reached by carefully studying the Holy Scriptures. Paradise was simply moved, and the Place of Torments remained.

There is one other scriptural assumption that is preached and taught in almost every church today, but in actuality has no biblical basis. In any church today, one might hear the pastor or priest make an uninstantiated statement that when a person dies, they are immediately taken to Heaven to live with God forever. The truth is that if one will carefully study the scriptures, there is not one shred of evidence that this statement can be proven or even suggested. A clergy or seminary professor might quote the following statements by the Apostle Paul as "proof".

[8] *We are confident, I say, and willing rather to be absent from the body, and to be present with the Lord.*
[9] *Wherefore we labor, that, whether present or absent, we may be accepted of him.*
                    II Corinthians 5:8-9
[21] *For to me to live is Christ, and to die is gain.*
[22] *But if I live in the flesh, this is the fruit of my labour: yet what I shall choose I wot not.*
[23] *For I am in a strait betwixt two, having a desire to depart, and to be with Christ; which is far better*   Philippians 1:21-23

Note carefully that there is no *immediacy* in Paul's statement. He is simply saying that he would rather be present with the Lord than to be in this earthly tabernacle. It is much like someone saying; *I would rather be fishing than to be at work today*. In this place called Paradise which now exists in the third heaven, all New Covenant believers join all of the Old Testament saints who were saved by *faith* and await the second advent of Jesus Christ. Paul is simply saying that he is willing and desires to be with the Lord rather than serving him on the earth. This is not a discourse of what immediately happens after death. In fact, taken in context with II Corinthians 5:8, Paul makes the following statement:

[9] *Wherefore we labor, that, whether present or absent, we may be accepted of him.*
[10] *For we must all appear before the judgment seat of Christ; that every one may receive the things done in his body, according to that he hath done, whether it be good or bad.*
                    II Corinthians 5:9-10

II Corinthians 5:9-10 immediately follows and is linked to II Corinthians 5:8. The *good or bad things* which Paul refers to these verses are without controversy referring to the *Bema Seat*

Judgment in which all Old Testament and New Testament believers will be judged according to their works for *rewards*, not *salvation*. This will not take place until after the 2nd advent of Christ which is now approaching 2000 years after Paul made these statements!!! So where has the soul of Paul been for these 2000 years?? He is in Paradise awaiting the Bema Seat Judgment.

If this reasonable and scripturally-based conclusion is correct…and I think that it is….notice that modern Pastors are not far from the truth. When a true believer dies today, that believer is transported into the 3rd heaven of God but not into His throne room. While not specifically stated, I believe that those now in Paradise can see God in all of His glory from afar, but will not enter into the third heaven until after the Bema Seat Judgment for rewards takes place after the Battle of Armageddon. This will be shown true in Chapter 6.

The real reason why I firmly believe that at death one's soul does not go immediately to God is that when those in faith die, it is beyond controversy that the dead in Christ will be resurrected from the grave and those alive in Christ will be raptured to Jesus Christ in the air at the last trump. There they will appear before God at the Bema Seat Judgment to receive their crowns of righteousness and their eternal rewards. No one doubts that this is true. Are we to believe that believers are already in heaven receiving rewards and assignments based upon works before the well documented judgment of rewards? If they are, what kind of heavenly body are they wearing? What kind of rewards have already been received? The entire scenario is beyond rational belief. It is not until Christ will return to gather all believers to him in the rapture of the living and the resurrection of the dead that souls will be given a celestial body. If true believers are already in heaven, this means that there really isn't much reason for Jesus Christ to return to take believers with Him to heaven; because all those that have believed in Him would already be in heaven.

Finally, when Jesus Christ returns for all of those dead and alive that have faith in Him, they will be given white robes, a new name, and they will be kings & priests with Him for a thousand years. What sense would all this make if the deceased are already in heaven and serving God? If someone dies and goes to heaven at death *before* the Last Bema Seat Judgment is held in heaven for rewards, what need is there for him to be judged for rewards at the 2^{cd} coming ? Hasn't that person already been rewarded if he/ she is already in heaven and serving Christ? One cannot be in the presence of the Lord until a new immortal, glorified, incorruptible body has been given to us by Christ after the *last trump* has sounded. It is time that we discarded popular theology and spoke the clear and logical truth of biblical scriptures. In reality, it really makes little difference because if one has to wait in Paradise for a few thousand years, this is a mere dot in the scope of eternity.

*….ye shall know the **truth**, and the **truth** shall make you free*   John 8:1

Where are the Unbelievers in Christ? Do they still exist in spirit form?

Today, when an *unbeliever* dies, he or she joins all Old Testament and New Testament unbelievers in the *torments* side of Sheol. At the final judgment, all souls residing there will be taken to the *Great White Throne Judgment*, where its occupants will be judged prior to being cast into the *Lake of Fire* (Revelation 20:13–15). This is 1000 years after all *believers* will have been judged; not for punishment but for rewards. This will take place at the *Bema Seat Judgment* immediately following the *resurrection* of all dead saints and the *rapture* of all those who remain alive. Paul knew the truth but could not disclose it after he was caught up into Paradise after the resurrection of Jesus Christ (II Corinthians 12:2-4). It is almost universally taught (correctly) that when a true believer dies, the soul of the departed is immediately taken into the third heaven, but until corruption is replaced by incorruption and the Bema Seat Judgment takes place one cannot enter into the immediate presence of God.

Note: The Catholic Church and others (incorrectly) teach that there is an intermediate state and place of existence called, *Purgatory* (Latin: Purgatorium) in which those destined for heaven "undergo purification", so as to "achieve the holiness necessary to enter the joys of heaven". There is no scriptural confirmation or teaching that supports this concept. In fact, it assumes that the sacrificial death of Jesus Christ and the free offer of eternal life by grace and not by works was not sufficient to offer permanent salvation. It appears that this heretical concept might have emerged because of a lack of understanding about Paradise.

Is the Soul Immortal?

Throughout this entire study, it has been assumed and then biblically supported that mortal man consists of a body, soul and spirit. When one dies, the body separates from the soul and spirit; it then is buried in the earth (or cremated) and vanishes by decay. The soul and the spirit is then separated, and the spirit part of man returns to God from which it came. God started the human race by creating Adam. God formed a perfect man from the dust of the earth and then breathed life into him with His breath, and man became a living soul.

And the LORD God formed man of the dust of the ground, and breathed into his nostrils the breath of life; and man became a living soul   Genesis 2:7

Paul later described the first man Adam as a *natural man*, and then the last man a *quickening spirit*.

[45] *And so it is written, The first man Adam was made a living soul; the last Adam was made a quickening spirit.*
[46] *Howbeit that was not first which is spiritual, but that which is natural; and afterward that which is spiritual.*   I Corinthians 15:45-46

Recall that the spiritual component of man is the communication center and the linkage to God. Adam needed no spiritual component, since he actually walked and talked with God. When Adam and Eve fell, them and everyone to follow possessed the sin nature, and God cannot be in the presence of sinful man. It was then necessary to put into mortal man a spiritual component. After the crucifixion and resurrection of Jesus Christ, He gave the Holy Spirit to anyone who would accept Him as Lord and Savior. Before the death of Jesus Christ, the spirit from God was given to all those that would obey the Laws of God; written or natural. That spirit was never called the Holy Spirit, but one might easily conjecture that it was the same spirit that now dwells in any New Testament believer.

Notice that there is no mention in the creation account of Adam being a *living spirit*. The spirit in man is the component of man that allows man to be in intimate contact with God, even though every person after Adam and Eve possessed a sin-nature in his mortal body. Hence, Adam and Eve walked, talked and communicated with God directly in the Garden of Eden. After the fall of Adam and Eve, mankind became alienated from God. To allow God to spiritually communicate with sinful man, He gave each person a spiritual component. A key verse that clearly establishes that the soul and spirit parts of man are separate components of man was given by in the great Book of Hebrews.

For the word of God is quick, and powerful, and sharper than any two edged sword, piercing even to the dividing asunder of soul and spirit, and of the joints and marrow, and is a discerner of the thoughts and intents of the heart Hebrews 4:12

This verse reveals to us two important truths about the *inner man*: (1). The soul and spirit are two different components of man and (2) The soul and spirit can be separated. We conclude this section by quoting from perhaps the most influential biblical scholar of modern times: John Calvin.

It is foolish and rash to inquire into hidden things, farther than God permits us to know. Scripture, after telling that Christ is present with them, and receives them into paradise (John 12:32), and that they are comforted, while the souls of the reprobate suffer the torments which they have merited goes no farther. What teacher or doctor will reveal to us what God has concealed? As to the place of abode, the question is not less futile and inept, since we know that the dimension of the soul is not the same as that of the body. When the abode of blessed spirits is designated as the Bosom of Abraham, it is plain that, on quitting this pilgrimage, they are received by the common father of the faithful, who imparts to them the fruit of his faith. Still, since scripture uniformly enjoins us to look with expectation to the advent of Christ, and delays the crown of glory till that period, let us be contented with the limits divinely prescribed to us---- that the souls of the righteous, after their warfare is ended, obtain blessed rest where in joy they wait for the fruition of promised glory, and that thus the final result is suspended till Christ the Redeemer appear. There can be no doubt that the reprobate have the same doom as that which Jude assigns to the devils, they are "reserved in everlasting chains under darkness unto the judgment of the great day," (Jude 6).

Holy Ghost or Holy Spirit ?

The terms Holy Ghost and Holy Spirit are sometimes taken to represent different components of the spiritual man. The term Holy Ghost is not found in any of the new modern bible translations, and only survives in the Authorized King James Bible. The term Holy Ghost appears 90 times in the KJV and the term Holy Spirit only 7 times. The use of these terms is rather unusual, since the Hebrew and Greek words for Ghost and Spirit are exactly the same (*Agios Pneuma*). It is clear that the KJV translators did not mean to imply the modern concept of a supernatural being called a ghost. In fact, the modern concept of a Casper-like ghost has no basis in the scriptures. It is certain that the KJV translators recognized that either term represented a spirit which is uniquely associated with God or it is a temporary spiritual state assigned to man to achieve a specific and special purpose Why the KJV translators chose to use two different terms for the same spirit is a mystery. The New Testament Biblical interpretation of the Holy Spirit is that (1) It was given to all true believers by Jesus Christ as a comforter to all who look forward to his 2nd coming (2) It was given for spiritual discernment and understanding and (3) It is a power gift that a Christian can use to defeat Satan and his demons.

When anyone places their faith and hope in Jesus Christ, they are born-again and receive the gift of the Holy Spirit. The Holy Spirit comes to live within us; He convicts us of our sins and convinces us of our need to commit our lives to Jesus Christ. Jesus said, *When he comes, he will convict the world of guilt in regard to sin and righteousness and judgment* (John 16:8). God has also given His Spirit to us to teach us and open our eyes to God's truth as it is found in His Holy Bible. Perhaps the most important attribute of the Holy Spirit is that it gives *9 gifts* of the Holy Spirit and *9 fruits* of the Holy Spirit.

Gifts of The Holy Spirit

The classic scriptural passage on *Gifts of the Holy Spirit* was given by the Apostle Paul in I Corinthians 12.

[7] *But the manifestation of the Spirit is given to every man to profit withal.*
[8] *For to one is given by the Spirit the word of wisdom; to another the word of knowledge by the same Spirit;*
[9] *To another faith by the same Spirit; to another the gifts of healing by the same Spirit;*
[10] *To another the working of miracles; to another prophecy; to another discerning of spirits;*

to another divers kinds of tongues; to another the interpretation of tongues:

[11] *But all these worketh that one and the selfsame Spirit, dividing to every man severally as he will.*

[12] *For as the body is one, and hath many members, and all the members of that one body, being many, are one body: so also is Christ*   I Corinthians 12:7-12

However, there are actually 24 gifts of the Holy Spirit which are found in the New Testament Epistles.

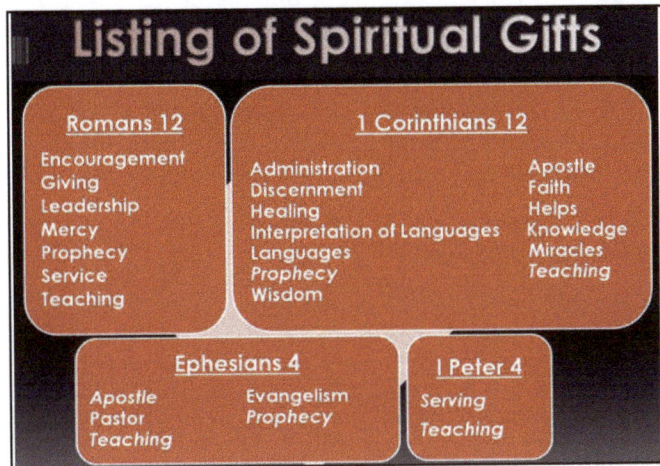

Listing of Spiritual Gifts

Romans 12
Encouragement
Giving
Leadership
Mercy
Prophecy
Service
Teaching

1 Corinthians 12
Administration
Discernment
Healing
Interpretation of Languages
Languages
Prophecy
Wisdom
Apostle
Faith
Helps
Knowledge
Miracles
Teaching

Ephesians 4
Apostle
Pastor
Teaching
Evangelism
Prophecy

I Peter 4
Serving
Teaching

Fruits of The Holy Spirit

The classic Biblical passage which describes *Holy Spirit Fruits* is given in the Apostle Paul's letter to the Galatians in which he lists 9 Fruits of the Spirit

[22] *But the fruit of the Spirit is love, joy, peace, longsuffering, gentleness, goodness, faith,*

[23] *Meekness, temperance: against such there is no* law   Galatians 5:22-23

Holy Spirit Fruits
1. Love
2. Joy
3. Peace
4. Longsuffering
5. Gentleness
6. Goodness
7. Faith
8. Meekness
9. Temperance

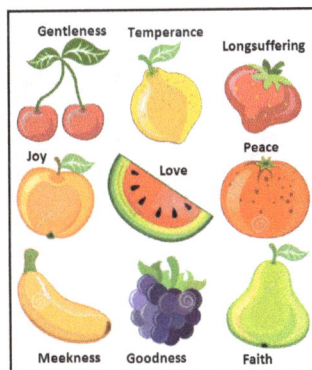

Each of the 24 *gifts* and 9 *fruits* of the Holy Spirit comes straight from God to us. The Holy Spirit is part of what we now call the *3-in-one*, which is composed of the Father, the Son and the Holy Spirit. How great is the God that we serve!! God the Father is allowing us to share in His

divine nature by giving to each of us these 18 qualities which allow us to serve him. It is generally true that every Christian can and should seek to exhibit each of the 9 *Fruits of the Spirit*, but the 9 *Gifts of the Holy Spirit* are made manifest in each born-again Christian as the Lord sees fit. The Gifts of the Holy Spirit is what distinguishes Christians in the *Body of Christ* from one another.

[4] *For as we have many members in one **body**, and all members have not the same office:*
[5] *So we, being many, are one **body** in Christ, and every one members one of another*
Romans 12:4-5

[12] *For as the **body** is one, and hath many members, and all the members of that one **body**, being many, are one **body**: so also is Christ.*
[13] *For by one Spirit are we all baptized into one **body**, whether we be Jews or Gentiles, whether we be bond or free; and have been all made to drink into one Spirit.*
[14] *For the **body** is not one member, but many.*
[15] *If the foot shall say, Because I am not the hand, I am not of the **body**; is it therefore not of the **body**?*
[16] *And if the ear shall say, Because I am not the eye, I am not of the **body**; is it therefore not of the **body**?*
[17] *If the whole **body** were an eye, where were the hearing? If the whole were hearing, where were the smelling?*
[18] *But now hath God set the members every one of them in the **body**, as it hath pleased him.*
[19] *And if they were all one member, where were the **body**?*
[20] *But now are they many members, yet but one **body**.*
[21]*And the eye cannot say unto the hand, I have no need of thee: nor again the head to the feet, I have no need of you.*
[22] *Nay, much more those members of the **body**, which seem to be more feeble, are necessary:*
[23] *And those members of the **body**, which we think to be less honorable, upon these we bestow more abundant honor; and our uncomely parts have more abundant comeliness.*
[24] *For our comely parts have no need: but God hath tempered the **body** together, having given more abundant honor to that part which lacked:*
[25] *That there should be no schism in the **body**; but that the members should have the same care one for another*   I Corinthians 12:12-25

The Holy Spirit

The average Christian in the denominational structures of modern religion will have a general knowledge of the Holy Spirit. There is no doubt that the Holy Spirit was promised to true believers by Jesus Christ in the latter days of His earthly ministry.

[16] *And I will pray the Father, and he shall give you another Comforter, that he may abide with you forever*
[17] *Even the Spirit of truth; whom the world cannot receive, because it seeth him not, neither knoweth him: but ye know him; for he dwelleth with you, and shall be in you.*

[26] *But the **Comforter**, which is the Holy Ghost, whom the Father will send in my name, he shall teach you all things, and bring all things to your remembrance, whatsoever I have said unto* you   John 14:16-17, 26

But when the Comforter is come, whom I will send unto you from the Father, even the Spirit of truth, which proceedeth from the Father, he shall testify of me   John 15:26

What is this *comforter* that Jesus Christ has promised will come? During His earthly ministry, Jesus taught and empowered His disciples to carry on His earthly ministry when He would depart from them. In John 14:16-26, He is preparing to leave them. He promises that God would give to them the Holy Spirit which would comfort them and take the place of His physical presence. Jesus called the Spirit *another Comforter*. In the Greek language this is *another of the same kind*. In John 14:26 Christ continues and calls this comforter the *Holy Ghost*, where the translators of the KJV have used the word ghost for spirit. This Holy Spirit which speaks truth is *not* identical to either the Son or the Father, but they are one and the same in holiness and purpose. It is not clear why the KJV translators sometimes used Holy Ghost and sometimes used Holy Spirit. The original Greek or Hebrew word can be recovered with a good concordance.

In the 13th century the Catholic church correctly promoted the concept that the spirit which lives in all true believers is the Holy Spirit, but incorrectly taught that the Father, Son and Holy Spirit are identical; three in one. It is definitely true that the Father and the son are both of one accord and one mind, but they are not the same. Christ himself said that:

*All things are delivered unto me of my **Father**: and no man knoweth the Son, but the **Father**; neither knoweth any man the **Father**, save the Son, and he to whomsoever the Son will reveal him*   Matthew 11:27

*The **Father** loveth the Son, and hath given all things into his hand*   John 3:35

Are we to believe that that the Father delivered and gave all things to Himself? The concept of the Father, Son and Holy Spirit existing as three manifestations of the same deity is false teaching which cannot be sustained by the Holy Scriptures.

Christ declared that He must go to the cross, die and depart from this world. He then promised that He would send another to take His place: He called this gift a *comforter*.

[16] *And I will pray the Father, and he shall give you another **Comforter**, that he may abide with you for ever;*
[26] *But the **Comforter**, which is the Holy Ghost, whom the Father will send in my name, he shall teach you all things, and bring all things to your remembrance, whatsoever I have said unto you*   John 14:16,26

31

*But when the **Comforter** is come, whom I will send unto you from the Father, even the Spirit of truth, which proceedeth from the Father, he shall testify of me*   John 15:26

*Nevertheless I tell you the truth; It is expedient for you that I go away: for if I go not away, the **Comforter** will not come unto you; but if I depart, I will send him unto you*   John 16:7

The Greek word translated *Comforter* or *Counselor* is *parakletos* and it is of masculine form. This properly means *one called to the side of another*; *one of the same kind*. The word also carries a secondary notion concerning the purpose of providing understanding: *to counsel or support the one who needs it* and to *speak truth*. This Comforter or *Paraclete* is a spiritual being, and He indwells every believer. The New Testament speaks of both the spirit and the Holy Spirit; sometimes The New Testament translators used the term *Holy Ghost*. in the Greek language, the terms Holy Ghost and Holy Spirit come from exactly the same root words. Further insight is given as to the internal and real presence of the Holy Spirit in all believers by the great theologian John MacArthur.

> The Holy Spirit is not a mystical power; He is a person just as Jesus is a person. He is not a floating fog or some kind of ghostlike emanation. It is unfortunate that the translators of the King James Version used the term *Ghost* instead of *Spirit*. For generations people have had the idea that the Holy Spirit is an apparition, something like Casper the Friendly Ghost, the 1950s and 60s comic book and cartoon character! But He's not a ghost; He's a person.
>
> All believers have two *paracletes*: the Spirit of God within us and the Son of God in heaven.   First John 2:1 says: *If anyone sins, we have an Advocate with the Father, Jesus Christ the righteous*. The Greek word translated "Advocate" is *parakletos*.

Authors Comment: You will note that in the preceding quotation that Dr. MacArthur refers to the Holy Spirit as a real person and as *he*, not an "it". This reflects the teaching of Scripture that the Holy Spirit is not just an impersonal force or a mere attribute of God's power, but rather a *spiritual person*. The Holy Spirit, just like all other angels and personages in Heaven were created by God and they are always referred to in the male gender. Many sects and cults teach otherwise, yet the use of the personal, masculine pronoun *he* for the Holy Spirit and the fact that the Spirit possesses a will, knowledge, power, understanding and affections reveals his person as a real, multipresent being created by God (John 16: 4–11; Ephesians 4:30). A real *mystery* concerning the Holy Spirit is that he is a singular being, but exists in multiple personages within each true believer. An atheist or nonbeliever will undoubtedly laugh at this notion and declare that such a multiple manifestation of the same being is clearly impossible. That is true in the secular word, but nothing is impossible for the God we serve. It is equally impossible for each

The Holy Spirit

Eternal Spirit (Hebrews 9:14)
Spirit of the Lord (Acts 5:9)
The Comforter (John 14:16)
Spirit of truth (John 14:17)
Spirit of understanding (Isaiah 11:2)
Spirit of wisdom (Ephesians 1:17)
Spirit of counsel (Isaiah 11:2)
Spirit of might (Isaiah 11:2)
Spirit of knowledge (Isaiah 11:2)
Breath of the Almighty (Job 33:4)
Spirit of holiness (Romans 1:4)

unbeliever to understand or accept the resurrection of the dead, existence after physical death and life eternal. The Holy Spirit is real and lives within each true believer.

We have a personal relationship with the Holy Spirit, just as we have a personal relationship with God the Father and God the Son. Christ spoke clearly of three distinct personages of God when commanding His disciples to evangelize the world. This should be enough evidence that the Holy Trinity is not 3 in 1 but 1 in 3.

Go ye therefore, and teach all nations, baptizing them in the name of the Father, and of the Son, and of the Holy Ghost   Matthew 28:19

When Saul of Tarsus was chosen by God and converted on the road to Damascus, he was sent blind to the house of Ananias where some say he stayed for up to 2 years. Ananias evidently was chosen to restore his sight and to prepare him for the gift of the Holy Spirit.

*And Ananias went his way, and entered into the house; and putting his hands on him said, Brother Saul, the Lord, even Jesus, that appeared unto thee in the way as thou camest, hath sent me, that thou mightest receive thy sight, and be filled with the **Holy** Ghost*   Acts 9:17

When Paul later went to Corinth and came to Ephesus, he spoke to a group of new Christians and asked them the following question.

[2] *He said unto them, Have ye received the **Holy** Ghost since ye believed? And they said unto him, We have not so much as heard whether there be any **Holy** Ghost.*
[6] *And when Paul had laid his hands upon them, the **Holy** Ghost came on them; and they spake with tongues, and prophesied*   Acts 19: 2,6

This was after Pentecost, and proves several important things: (1) A Christian can awaken the power of the Holy Ghost (Holy Spirit) upon another Christian. (2) Paul establishes the validity of laying hands upon someone to impart the Holy Spirit (3) A Christian can be active in serving Christ without the personal indwelling of the Holy Spirit (4) The Holy Spirit can institute and manifest evidence of its presence, such as speaking in tongues and prophesying. It is clear that the Holy Spirit can bring with it multiple gifts which unbelievers do not possess in the same magnitude. The presence and indwelling of the Holy Ghost/Holy Spirit is Biblically proven, both before and after the Day of Pentecost, but does the work of the Holy Spirit extend into the Old Testament?

Old Testament Holy Spirit

Many pastors and theologians will preach that the Holy Spirit came and fell on believers on the Day of Pentecost and that the Holy Spirit would bring understanding, wisdom, support and power upon every Christian on the day that they were born again into the Body of Christ. It is true that every born-again Christian receives the Gift of the Holy Spirit, but possession and indwelling of the Holy Spirit is not limited to that particular spiritual rebirth. The Holy Spirit was in John the Baptist when he was yet an infant in the womb of Elizabeth (Luke 1:15). Both Elizabeth and Zachariah were filled immediately with the Holy ghost when they heard that Mary would be the mother of Jesus (Luke 1:41,67).

It is clear to all Jews and Christians that God is the same today, yesterday and tomorrow: He is omnipresent, omnipotent, holy and unchanging. The role of the Holy Spirit in the Old Testament was not principally different from the role of the Holy Spirit in the New Testament.

While there are some differences, there's an undeniable unity between the two Testaments. Old Testament men and women, both *before* the Law was given at Mt. Sinai and *after* the law was put into effect by God in 1490 BC, had no knowledge whatsoever of the *New* Testament. To them the Hebrew Bible was never *old.* It is only through the New Testament writings that details of the work and person of Jesus Christ in the Old Testament were revealed and understood. The fulfillment of ancient Messianic prophecies pertaining to Jesus Christ of Nazareth finally came to pass, and the Holy Spirit was given by that name by Jesus Christ. It was promised to all believers by Christ when He ascended to His Father in heaven, and it fell 50 days later on the Day of Pentecost on 6000 believers. It is only through the further revelation of the New Testament that we come to the full glory, grandeur, and power of the Holy Spirit's role, relationships, work, and gifts. However, the same Holy Spirit was active and present in many ways throughout the Old Testament; it was just not called the Holy Spirit. As we study the Old Testament, we see that the *Spirit* was given to many individuals to help fulfill the plan of God. When the Bible speaks of any creative act, the Spirit's work in creation is always mentioned. When conquest is being

The Holy Spirit Ministry in the Old Testament		
Num.	11:16-26	Seventy prophesy when the Spirit was put on them.
	24:1-6	Spirit comes on Balaam and he gives a prophet's blessing.
Judges	3:9-10	Spirit of the LORD comes upon Othniel.
	6:34	Spirit of the LORD "clothed" Gideon.
	11:29	Spirit of the LORD caused Jephthah to pass through Gilead and Manasseh.
	13:25	Spirit of the LORD began to stir in Samson.
	15:14	Spirit of the LORD came upon him mightily so that the ropes that were on his arms were as flax that is burned with fire, and his bonds dropped from his hands.
1 Sam.	10:6-10	Spirit of the LORD came upon Samuel mightily, and he prophesied.
	16:13-14	Spirit of the LORD came mightily upon David from that day forward.
	19:20-23	Spirit of God came upon the messengers of Saul, and they also prophesied.

described, His work in empowering men for battle is recorded. When the tabernacle is being built, His impartation of wisdom to craftsmen is given to ordinary men. The Holy Spirit is very much involved in the works of all Old Testament believers. Jesus was addressing a Pharisee called Nicodemus who was a ruler of the Jews (John 3:1-9). Jesus informed him that any man cannot receive salvation unless he is born of both the spirit and the water. Nicodemus did not understand, and Jesus replied :

Art thou a master of Israel, and knowest not these things?   John 3:10

Jesus is plainly stating that if Nicodemus was a Jew, how could he not understand the role of the Spirit/Holy Spirit in salvation. This and other passages clearly indicate that the Old Testament Jews was well aware of the spirit sent to man from God. A fruit of the Spirit's regenerating work is greater faith (Ephesians 2:8). We know that there were men of faith in the Old Testament because the *great faith chapter* of Hebrews 11 names many of them. If faith is increased and made sure by the regenerating power of the Holy Spirit, then this must have been the case for Old Testament saints who looked ahead to the cross, believing that what God had promised in regard to their redemption that would come to pass. In some ways, the true faith of Abraham and the other Old Testament men of faith might have been stronger than a believer today since they looked forward to things not yet made manifest, and we have the advantage of the New Testament writings and looking backwards.

[1] *Now faith is the substance of things hoped for, the evidence of things not **seen**.*
[3] *Through faith we understand that the worlds were framed by the word of God, so that things which are **seen** were not made of things which do appear.*
[7] *By faith Noah, being warned of God of things not **seen** as yet, moved with fear, prepared an ark to the saving of his house; by the which he condemned the world, and became heir of the righteousness which is by faith.*
[13] *These all died in faith, not having received the promises, but having **seen** them afar off, and were persuaded of them, and embraced them, and confessed that they were strangers and pilgrims on the earth*   Hebrews 11:1, 3, 7, 13

The primary aspect of the Spirit's work in the Old Testament was that it was not given as part of a covenant promise, but that it was given to accomplish things that mortal men could not. This is the major difference between the Spirit's role in the Old and the New Testament. Both were given by God, but in the Old Testament God was dealing with true believers personally, and in the New Testament through His Son Jesus Christ. One (OT) was a true gift, the other was a gift and a promise (NT). The New Testament teaches the permanent indwelling of the Holy Spirit in *all* believers (1 Corinthians 3:16-17; 6:19-20) as a *guarantee of our inheritance* (Ephesians 1:13-14). When we place our faith in Jesus Christ for salvation, the Holy Spirit comes to live within us. The Apostle Paul calls this *permanent indwelling*, in contrast to the Old Testament in which the indwelling of the spirit was selective and usually temporary. The Spirit *came upon* such Old Testament people as Joshua (Numbers 27:18), David (1 Samuel 16:12-13) and even Saul (1 Samuel 10:10). In the book of Judges, we see the Spirit *coming upon* selective judges who God raised up to deliver Israel from their oppressors. The spirit came upon these individuals for specific tasks and to equip them for specific assignments and responsibilities. The indwelling of the spirit was a sign of God's favor upon that individual, and if God's favor left an individual;

the spirit would depart also. (Saul in 1 Samuel 16:14). The spirit coming upon an individual doesn't always guarantee that the person might not fall into a sinful state. (consider Sampson).

People in the Old testament received the spirit just as people in the New Testament received the Holy Spirit, but it was by God's own choosing. It is possible and even likely that the spirit given in the Old Testament was the same as the Holy Spirit in the New Testament. . David needed the supernatural power of God just as much as the apostle Paul needed it. People received power through the Holy Spirit in the same measure throughout the Old and New Testaments, and one cannot be given divine power except that it comes from God, who co-exists a Holy Trinity; Father, Son and Holy Ghost (spirit). Although the Father, Son and the Holy Spirit exists *as three in one* in nature, character and purpose (II Corinthians 13:14, Matthew 28:19); they are *not* one manifestation in 3 parts; they are distinct individuals that are all in agreement (one). We serve only one God that is revealed to us in three distinct persons: the Father, the Son, and the Holy Spirit.

[6] *This is he that came by water and blood, even Jesus Christ; not by water only, but by water and blood. And it is the Spirit that beareth witness, because the Spirit is truth.*
[7] *For there are three that bear record in heaven, the Father, the Word, and the Holy Ghost: and these three are one*   I John 5:6-7

Jesus said that He wasn't the Father more than 80 times. While always remaining one in purpose and origin, Jesus and the Father are clearly separate and distinct persons. This is made clear in the Gospel of John when Christ was baptized in the River Jordan.

[16] *And Jesus, when he was baptized, went up straightway out of the water: and, lo, the heavens were opened unto him, and he saw the Spirit of God descending like a dove, and lighting upon him:*
[17] *And lo a voice from heaven, saying, This is my beloved Son, in whom I am well pleased*
          Matthew 3:16-17

Note that as a man, Jesus Christ received the Spirit of God in full measure. In his great sermon to the scribes and Pharisees which resulted in his death, Stephen made the following statement.

You stiff-necked and uncircumcised in heart and ears! You always resist the Holy Spirit; as your fathers did, so do you   Acts 7:51

John Mark recorded the following statement by Jesus Christ as He taught in Herod's Temple.

For David himself said by the Holy Spirit: The Lord said to my Lord, sit at My right hand, till I make Your enemies Your footstool.   Mark 12:36

This is an often overlooked but incredible statement! *First*, King David is well aware that there is a Holy Spirit. *Second*, the utterance of King David in this verse was revealed to him by the Holy Spirit. *Third*, David had knowledge long ago that there was a Lord (Jesus Christ) sitting next the Lord (Jehovah) in the heavenly throne room (The Lord said to my Lord), *Fourth*, this was prophetic of when all the enemies of Jesus Christ will be defeated sometime long after he was dead and buried. These two witnesses confirm that men of faith in the Old Testament knew that there was a Holy Spirit. It is beyond controversy that King David knew of the gift of the Holy Spirit to him.

*Cast me not away from thy presence; and take not thy **holy spirit** from me*   Psalms 51:11

Summary and Conclusions

The Holy Spirit will function in different roles at different times, but as the third Person of the Trinity, His nature is always the same. The same Spirit involved in the creation of the universe lives within those who follow Christ today. Christians today enjoy the daily benefit of a personal relationship with God through the presence of the Holy Spirit. Old Testament saints were given the Holy Spirit (spirit) by God to accomplish specific goals or to carry out specific assignments. The Spirit who strengthened Samson and caused David to dance now empowers us and fills us with joy: *Not by might nor by power, but by My Spirit, says the LORD of hosts* (Zechariah 4:6).

Biblical evidence strongly supports the conclusion that the *physical* man (body) is mortal and perishable, while the *spiritual man* (soul and spirit) is immortal. At death, the physical *body* will die and return to the dust from which it was formed by God; the *spirit* part of man returns to God from which it came and; the *soul* of man either passes directly to Paradise or to a Place of Torments. Anyone who has believed that God would find a way to both forgive their sins and offer salvation by a promised Messiah (Old Testament), or has been born-again under the New Covenant, will be given a new incorruptible body and ascend to heaven with Christ at the last trump, and each will be rewarded at the *Bema Seat Judgment*. The soul of the unregenerate sinner who has never been saved by *faith* will be cast into Gehenna or the Lake of Fire 1000 years later at the *Great White Throne judgment*.

There is no fundamental difference in what happened to the Old testament *Believers* and the New Testament *believers* at death. In both the Old and New Testament, all believers were taken to a place called Paradise which was also called Abraham's Bosom. This was a subterranean compartment in the heart of the earth during Old Testament times. Paradise was evidently moved into the 3rd heaven by Jesus Christ after He visited those being held there for 3 days and 3 nights. From where it was placed, the glory of God and His throne could be seen, which was a visible promise of things yet to come. Since the New Covenant began with the sacrificial death and ascension of Christ to His Father, all New Testament saints now also reside in Paradise awaiting the Bema Seat Judgment (Chapter 6).

The Souls *of All Unbelievers* from both the Old and New Testament were transported to a Place of Torments, where they await their final Judgment at the Great White Throne Judgment following the 1000 year Millennial Kingdom. Before the resurrection of Christ, Both Paradise and the Place of Torments were contained in a place called Gehenna (Hebrew) or Hades (Greek).

Sheol or Hades

The *First Death*

A Place of Torments

The Place where all unbelievers are being Held awaiting Final Judgment

A Great Gulf that None can Cross

Paradise

The Abode of All Righteous Believers from the Old Testament and all New Testament Believers

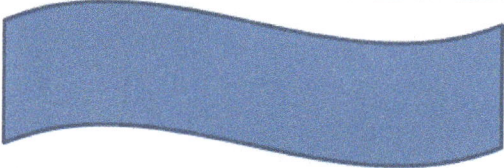

(Abraham's Bosom)

New Testament

Paradise

The Abode of All Righteous Believers from the Old Testament and all New Testament Believers

(Abraham's Bosom)

A Place of Torments

The Place where all unbelievers are being Held awaiting Final Judgment

Chapter 3

The Subterranean Compartments Which Hold Fallen Angels

There are three heavens which are described in the Holy Scriptures. There is the *3rd heaven* (II Corinthians 12:2) which is where God dwells with all of his *Holy Angels*. The *2nd heaven* is the galaxies and stars which surround the earth, and the *1st heaven* is the atmosphere and clouds which envelop the planet earth. Satan is the god of this world (II Corinthians 4:4) who rules and reigns over all of his demonic forces. Satan (Lucifer) was cast out of heaven when he rebelled against God, but for reasons only known to God he is still allowed access to the throne of God (Job 2:1), where he accuses the saints of evil deeds (Revelation 12:10). The angels which serve Satan are referred to as *demons*. They roam the earth seeking to find a body in which to live (Mark 5). Angels appear to be confined to this earth, or more accurately they have been banned from heaven.

The angels which followed after Satan and were cast out of heaven were not the only group of angels that rebelled against God. God has designated dungeons in the lower parts of the earth that hold several groups of angels who are not allowed to roam free upon this earth, but are being held in a state of consciousness awaiting their final judgment and sentencing. There are three compartments of incarceration that seem to be somewhere in the lowest part of the earth. (1) A place called *Abussos* which is also called the Bottomless Pit or the Abyss. (2) *Gehenna* or the Lake of Burning Fire and (3) a place called *Tartorus*.

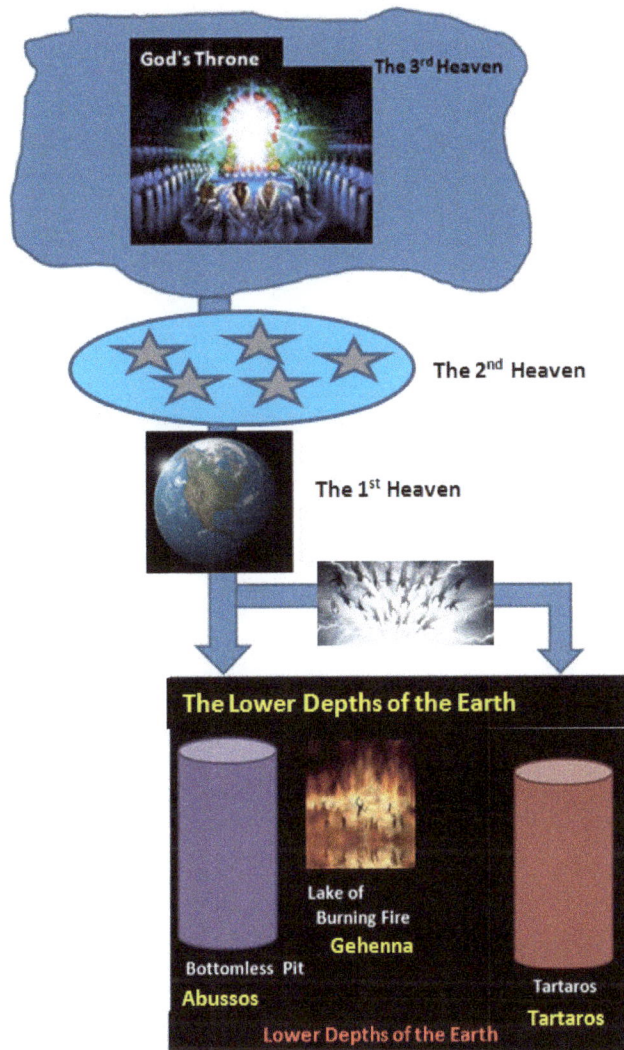

Abussos

The Greek word ἄβυσσος is directly translated as *Abussos,* which literally means the *bottomless pit*; "deep" or "bottomless". Abussos occurs 9 times in the *Septuagint* (LXX) Greek New Testament. The Greek word Abussos does not directly appear in the Authorized King James Version: the KJV Greek translators used the words "deep" in two cases and the phrase bottomless pit in nine cases. Other modern versions of the Bible frequently use the word *Abyss* for Abussos.

Translation of Greek word *Abussos* in King James Version of the Bible	
Luke 8:31	Deep
Romans 10:7	Deep
Revelation 9:1	Bottomless Pit
Revelation 9:1	Bottomless Pit
Revelation 9:2	Bottomless Pit
Revelation 9:11	Bottomless Pit
Revelation 11:7	Bottomless Pit
Revelation 17:8	Bottomless Pit
Revelation 20:1	Bottomless Pit
Revelation 20:3	Bottomless Pit

Abussos is evidently in the subterranean areas of the earth. It is the place of incarceration for a special class of angels which look like *locusts*, who are being held there until the 6th trumpet sounds in the Great Tribulation period. At that time, they will be released to torment mankind for 5 months. There are so many of these demon angels, that when they are released they will darken the light of the sun.

[1] *And the fifth angel sounded, and I saw a star fall from heaven unto the earth: and to him was given the key of the bottomless pit.*

[2] *And he opened the bottomless pit; and there arose a smoke out of the pit, as the smoke of a great furnace; and the sun and the air were darkened by reason of the smoke of the pit.*

[3] *And there came out of the smoke locusts upon the earth: and unto them was given power, as the scorpions of the earth have power.*

[4] *And it was commanded them that they should not hurt the grass of the earth, neither any green thing, neither any tree; but only those men which have not the seal of God in their foreheads.*

[5] *And to them it was given that they should not kill them, but that they should be tormented five months: and their torment was as the torment of a scorpion, when he striketh a man.*

[6] *And in those days shall men seek death, and shall not find it; and shall desire to die, and death shall flee from them*   Revelation 9:1-6

These locust-demons will have a king or a ruler over them called *Abaddon* (Hebrew) or *Apollyon* (Greek).

And they had a king over them, which is the angel of the bottomless pit, whose name in the Hebrew tongue is Abaddon, but in the Greek tongue hath his name Apollyon   Revelation 9:11

How or when Abaddon and the locust-creatures these were placed into the Abyss is not revealed in scriptures. In addition to these demonic forces, it seems that there will be ordinary demons periodically cast into the Abyss. In Luke 8:26-30 it is written that Jesus Christ visited a place called the country of the *Gadarenes*, where He encountered a man who was completely controlled by demons living in his body. Jesus had mercy on this man and He cast the demons out of the man's body. The demons were terrified at what had happened and they begged Jesus not to send them down into the *abyss*. They asked Jesus to permit them to inherit a herd of swine, which they did. The swine were so tormented that they *ran off into a lake and drowned.*

[26] *And they arrived at the country of the Gadarenes, which is over against Galilee.*

[27] *And when he went forth to land, there met him out of the city a certain man, which had devils long time, and ware no clothes, neither abode in any house, but in the tombs.*

[28] *When he saw Jesus, he cried out, and fell down before him, and with a loud voice said, What have I to do with thee, Jesus, thou Son of God most high? I beseech thee, torment me not.*

[29] *(For he had commanded the unclean spirit to come out of the man. For oftentimes it had caught him: and he was kept bound with chains and in fetters; and he brake the bands, and was driven of the devil into the wilderness.)*

[30] *And Jesus asked him, saying, What is thy name? And he said, Legion: because many devils were entered into him.*

[31] ***And they besought him that he would not command them to go out into the deep*** *(Abyss)*

[32] *And there was there an herd of many swine feeding on the mountain: and they besought him that he would suffer them to enter into them. And he suffered them.*

[33] *Then went the devils out of the man, and entered into the swine: and the herd ran violently down a steep place into the lake, and were choked (drowned)*   Luke 8:26-33

The bottomless pit is also where a particularly evil spirit is being held until it is called out during the great tribulation period of 3.5 years. This powerful and evil angel is called a *beast* (Revelation 11:7-8). It is believed that this beast will arise from out of the Abyss, completely take over a human body, and serve Satan as an individual which has been called the *Antichrist*.

The scenario is complicated (See Phillips, *Revelation: Mysteries Revealed*), but this particular, powerful angel will inhabit the body of a great world leader who will arise in the end times after he has been *wounded unto death* by a large knife or sword. After the angel takes over the body of this great world leader, he will be known as the ultimate *Antichrist* who will execute great persecution of all the Jews and Christians who are upon the earth (Revelation 13:1-10). This *beast* will not only persecute all Jews and Christians, but will kill two witnesses that stand in the rebuilt temple in Jerusalem to testify and warn people not to worship the beast or to take the mark of the beast (666).

[7] *And when they shall have finished their testimony, the beast that ascendeth out of the*
    bottomless pit *shall make war against them, and shall overcome them, and kill them.*
[8] *And their dead bodies shall lie in the street of the great city, which spiritually is called Sodom and Egypt, where also our Lord was crucified*   Revelation 11:7-8

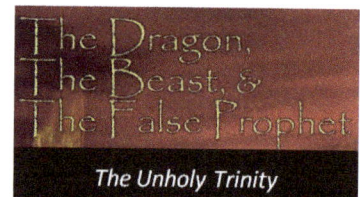

This same beast is fully empowered by Satan. This beast is also seen in Revelation 17:8 as carrying the False Prophet, who is depicted as an adulterous woman bedecked in scarlet robes, gold and jewels. She offers a one-world religion which denies Jesus Christ and obeys Satan.

When the *beast* who is the *antichrist* finishes his reign of 3.5 years, he, Satan and the false prophet will be defeated at the *Battle of Armageddon*. This Battle will shortly be followed by the 1000 year Millennial Kingdom. Before this 1000 year period begins, an angel will come down from Heaven with a key to the *Bottomless Pit* or the *Abyss*. (Revelation 20:1-2). This mighty angel will seize Satan and cast him down into the Pit where he will be *bound*. The *beast* and the *False Prophet* will be cast into the Lake of Fire.

[19] *And I saw the beast, and the kings of the earth, and their armies, gathered together to make war against him that sat on the horse, and against his army.*
[20] *And the beast was taken, and with him the false prophet that wrought miracles before him, with which he deceived them that had received the mark of the beast, and them that worshipped his image. These both were cast alive into a lake of fire burning with brimstone*   Revelation 19:19-20

After the 2^{cd} advent of Christ and the Battle of Armageddon, Satan is bound and shut up in the Bottomless Pit where he will remain for 1000 years until the Millennial Kingdom has run its course. At that time, he will be released for a short time (Revelation 20:7-8) to gather all of the wicked people from the earth who have committed sin and chosen to disobey God during this period of time. Satan will once again gather all of his forces (Revelation 20:8) outside of Jerusalem in the same place that the Battle of Armageddon took place 1000 years earlier (Satan never gives up!). The end will come swiftly as God destroys Satan and all of his followers. Satan is immediately cast into the *Lake of Burning Fire* where he is tormented forever. All of the men and women who joined him and were defeated at this last great battle will then be judged at the *Great White Throne Judgment* (Revelation 20:11-15).

Gehenna

In the depths of the earth (down) there is a place called *Gehenna* or the *Lake of Burning Fire*. In Jewish Rabbinic literature, and Christian and Islamic scripture, Gehenna is a destination of the wicked. This is a different place than Sheol/Hades which contains Paradise and the Place of Torments. The Greek word γηννα is literally *Gehenna,* and it occurs in the King James Translation of the *Septuagint* twelve times and is always translated as *hell*.

Lake of Burning Fire

Matthew 5:22	Matthew 5:29	Matthew 5:30	Matthew 10:28	Matthew 18:9
Matthew 23:15	Matthew 23:33	Mark 9:43	Mark 9:45	Mark 9:47
Luke 12:5	James 3:6			

The Lake of Burning Fire is only mentioned in the Book of Revelation (Revelation 19:20, 20:10, & 20:14-15). It is a place of eternal punishment for all unrepentant and fallen angels, and unbelievers of all ages (Matthew 25:41). It is described as a place of *burning sulfur*, and those who will be cast into it after the Great White Throne judgment will experience eternal, unspeakable agony of an unrelenting nature (Luke 16:24; Mark 9:45-46). All Old Testament unbelievers and all New Testament men or women who have rejected Christ are now being held in the temporary compartment called torments; which is one of the two divisions of *Hades/Sheol*. The Lake of Fire is their final destination.

We will now tread on ground which is rarely studied and poorly understood with few scriptural clues. Although some theologians do not identify the Lake of Fire as an actual place, this is clearly incorrect as we have just shown. The scriptures reveal that it is an actual place. The Holy Scriptures reveal that the lake of fire is directly associated with the *second death* (Revelation 20:14, 21:8). The *first death* resulted from Adam's sin and is a physical. This death can be overcome by resurrection from the dead (I Corinthians 15). The lake of fire represents a different or second kind of death. Once one is cast into the Lake of Fire, the second death takes place (Revelation 20:10-15). There is a raging theological debate over whether or not the result is a cessation or termination of life, or whether the Lake of Fire torments that angel or person forever. It is certain that Satan the Antichrist, and the False Prophet are cast into the Lake of Fire where they will be *tortured forever* (Revelation 20:10). It is also certain that at the Sheep and Goat judgment of Christ that the goat nations (people) will be cast into the Lake of Burning Fire (Matthew 25:31-33,41). Notice that Satan is an angelic creation, while the False Prophet and the Antichrist will be satanically controlled mortal men. It is also certain that anyone who's name is not found in God's *Book of Life* will be cast into the Lake of Fire on the last day at the *Great White Throne Judgment* (Revelation 20:1-15). It is also clear that there is no hope of ever recovering from the 2nd death. The Bible says that Jesus has the *keys of hell and of death* (Revelation 1:18), showing that he has the authority to release people from the 1st death brought about by Adam's sin and He has authority to condemn unbelievers to the 2^{cd} death. However, the scriptures never indicate that either Jesus nor anyone else has a key to the Lake of Fire. Once condemned to the Lake of Fire there is no escape forever. We will later show beyond any reasonable doubt that one thing is certain: all who put their trust and faith in Jesus Christ, and is born again, will not need to be afraid of whatever fate is represented by the second death and the Lake of Burning Fire.

Tartarus

Before the great flood, a group of angels came down to earth and cohabitated with women.

[4] There were giants in the earth in those days; and also after that, when the sons of God came in unto the daughters of men, and they bare children to them, the same became mighty men which were of old, men of renown.

[5] And GOD saw that the wickedness of man was great in the earth, and that every imagination of the thoughts of his heart was only evil continually.

[6] And it repented the LORD that he had made man on the earth, and it grieved him at his heart.

[7] And the LORD said, I will destroy man whom I have created from the face of the earth; both man, and beast, and the creeping thing, and the fowls of the air; for it repenteth me that I have made them.

[8] But Noah found grace in the eyes of the LORD   Genesis 6:4-8

The result was an offspring of giants called *Nephilim*. It is certain that Satan put this idea into this group of angels to try and corrupt the *Seed of Woman* in an attempt to negate the messianic prophecy of Genesis 3:15. This act was so offensive to God that it was one of the main reasons for the great flood which drowned all living land creatures except those saved by the ark of Noah. As punishment for their sin,, God cast every angel involved into a subterranean prison called *Tartarus*. Tartarus is evidently in the lower depths of the earth, and the angels which are being held there await the final judgment and fate which will be pronounced by God (II Peter 2:4). They are being *bound in chains* in complete *darkness* (Jude 6). When Christ returns at His

2nd advent, He will sit in judgment after the 1000 years millennial kingdom at the Great White Throne. The word Tartarus is only found once in the entire Bible, and that is in the Book of Peter.

For if God spared not the angels that sinned, but cast them down to hell, and delivered them into chains of darkness, to be reserved unto judgment II Peter 2:4

The word translated *hell* in the KJV is *Tartorus*. It is clear that the place called *Tartorus* is not the same as Sheol (Hebrew)/Hades(Greek). It has been suggested from ancient writings that Tartarus is a place of darkness and torments with flames of fire providing the only light.

It is generally recognized that Jude 6 also speaks of Tartorus and provides additional details.

And the angels which kept not their first estate, but left their own habitation, he hath reserved in everlasting chains under darkness unto the judgment of the great day Jude 1:6

Summary

In the Old Testament, the Hebrew word used to describe the realm of the dead is *sheol*. The New Testament Greek word for sheol is *Hades*. It simply means *the place of the dead* or the *place of departed souls/spirits*. To the Hebrews and later the Israelites, sheol was the place where all souls went upon death, and it was composed of two distinct compartments: *Paradise* and a *Place of Torments*. Paradise is also called *Abraham's Bosom* in Luke 16:23 Paradise was where the souls of all *believers* who were righteous and died in the faith of Abraham were taken by angels. Several Scriptures in the New Testament confirm that sheol/Hades is a temporary place where souls are kept as they await the final resurrection (Luke 23:43; 2 Corinthians 5:8; Philippians 1:23). The Place of Torments was the compartment where the souls of all *unbelievers* were transported. The prophet Daniel referred to these two places when he wrote:

[1] *And at that time shall Michael stand up, the great prince which stands for the children of thy people: and there shall be a time of trouble, such as never was since there was a nation even to that same time: and at that time thy people shall be delivered, every one that shall be found written in the book.*

[2] *And many of them that sleep in the dust of the earth shall awake, some to everlasting life, and some to shame and everlasting contempt.*

[3] *And they that be wise shall shine as the brightness of the firmament; and they that turn many to righteousness as the stars forever and ever*   Daniel 12:1-3

The phrase *that time* is when Satan will be cast out of heaven by Michael and his angels, and the great tribulation period will begin for 3.5 years. During this period of time, the Nation of Israel will realize that Jesus Christ is the redeemer which was promised long ago to Adam, Abraham and King David. *Sleep* was a generic word used in the Old Testament for death.

Daniel prophesies that many who *sleep* will be raised to *everlasting life,* and others *to shame and everlasting contempt.* These two resurrections of the dead are separated by the 1000 year Millennial Kingdom; The righteous will be resurrected at the rapture to be rewarded at the Bema Seat Judgment, and the unrighteous will be raised to be condemned to the Burning Lake of Fire at the Great White Throne Judgment. The righteous Old Testament dead will be raised along with the New Testament saints at the *Rapture.* Paul referred to the Daniel prophecy when he addressed the salvation of the Jews in his letter to the Romans.

[25] *For I would not, brethren, that ye should be ignorant of this mystery, lest ye should be wise in your own conceits; that blindness in part is happened to Israel, until the fullness of the Gentiles be come in.*
[26] *And so all Israel shall be saved: as it is written, There shall come out of Sion the Deliverer, and shall turn away ungodliness from Jacob:*
[27] *For this is my covenant unto them, when I shall take away their sins*   Romans 11:25-27

The Lord will make all of this happen because of His love for His chosen people.

[7] *Let Israel hope in the LORD: for with the LORD there is mercy, and with him is plenteous redemption.*
[8] *And he shall redeem Israel from all his iniquities*   Psalms 130:7-8

The compartment called *Gehenna* or the *Burning Lake of Fire* is mentioned only in Revelation 19:20 and 20:10, 14-15. The Greek word *Gehenna* is always translated as *hell* in the New Testament. It is the final destination of all unbelievers: a place of *eternal* punishment for: (1) Satan, Lucifer, the Antichrist and the False Prophet (2) Death and Hell (Revelation 20:14) (3) all fallen and demonic angels (4) all Old Testament nonbelievers who died in sin (5) those New Testament nonbelievers who refused to accept Jesus Christ as their Lord And Savior (6) those who remain alive after the Tribulation Period who showed no mercy and love to *His Brethren* during the worldwide persecution of Jews and Christians: These are called are called "goats" in Matthew 25:30-45. Gehenna is described as a place of burning sulfur, and those in it experience eternal, unspeakable agony of an unrelenting nature (Luke 16:24; Mark 9:45-46). The souls of all dead unbelievers are in the temporary abode of the dead called Hades/sheol, and are destined To the Lake of Burning Fire where they will be tormented forever (Revelation 20:15).

Those whose names are written in God's Book of Life or in the Lamb's Book of life have no fear of this terrible fate. Only by faith in Jesus Christ and by His blood that was shed on the cross of Calvary for our sins, we are destined to live eternally in the presence of God.

Chapter 4
Satan and His Demonic Followers

Adam and Eve were created by God and He placed them in the Garden of Eden to live in perfect communion with Him. They were given everything necessary to sustain life perpetually. Every tree was *pleasant* and grew fruit (Genesis 1:29), and in the Garden of Eden grew the *Tree of Life* (Genesis 2:9). Adam and Eve had no clear knowledge of good and evil, only the innocence and peace that can only be achieved without the corrupting impact of sin. Satan had long ago rebelled against God, and was cast out of the 3rd heaven where God and His holy angels dwell. Incredibly, when Lucifer was cast out of heaven, 1/3 of all the angels which God had created followed after him and worshipped him (Revelation 12:4). Satan or Lucifer has tremendous power and influence. His source of power is threefold: (1) He has his own power by virtue of how God made him. Satan was created with the highest power and beauty of any other angelic being.

[12] *Son of man, take up a lamentation upon the king of Tyrus, and say unto him, Thus saith the Lord GOD; Thou sealest up the sum, full of wisdom, and perfect in beauty.*

[13] *Thou hast been in Eden the garden of God; every precious stone was thy covering, the sardius, topaz, and the diamond, the beryl, the onyx, and the jasper, the sapphire, the emerald, and the carbuncle, and gold: the workmanship of thy tabrets and of thy pipes was prepared in thee in the day that thou wast created.*

[14] *Thou art the anointed cherub that covereth; and I have set thee so: thou wast upon the holy mountain of God; thou hast walked up and down in the midst of the stones of fire.*

[15] *Thou wast perfect in thy ways from the day that thou wast created, till iniquity was found in thee.*

[16] *By the multitude of thy merchandise they have filled the midst of thee with violence, and thou hast sinned: therefore I will cast thee as profane out of the mountain of God: and I will destroy thee, O covering cherub, from the midst of the stones of fire.* Ezekiel 28:12-16

(2) Satan has power over man by virtue of the fact that he deceived Adam and Eve and brought sin into their life. This was the single most destructive act ever perpetrated upon mankind. Because Adam sinned against God, he placed the curse of sin upon every man and woman that would ever be born. Mankind from that point on would be born with a *sin nature* in which the flesh would by heredity prefer acts of sinfulness over the holiness of God (Romans 6:6). Hence, the choice to follow after Jesus Christ today and live a righteous life is just that… a choice between good and evil.

(3) Satan has been imputed power over this earth by God. This is difficult to understand, but the reason is clear if each individual realizes that the choice of salvation and eternal life is again a *choice*. God has provided a path to salvation through His only Son, Jesus Christ. The sin issue was settled on the cross of Calvary and salvation is now based upon only one thing: Faith in the saving Grace of Jesus Christ and accepting Him as their redeemer, Lord and Savior. God will never force salvation and eternal life on anyone. it is an individual choice and is given freely by grace. Satan has power in this world, but it is limited and is allowed by God to exercise his influence on man. This is no more evident than during the 3.5 year period of time called the *Great Tribulation* during which the archangel Michael will *stand aside* to enable Satan, the Antichrist and the false prophet to persecute all Jews and Christians. Michael is the great angelic protector of Israel; it is no mystery that Israel as God's chosen people has never ceased to exist since God called them forth through the loins of Abraham. In Daniel 11 the prophet has been given a prophecy of the tribulation that Israel will experience in a time now revealed to us as the Great Tribulation. In Daniel 12:1 it is prophesied that during the Tribulation period, Michael will stand aside.

And at that time shall Michael stand up, the great prince which standeth for the children of thy people: and there shall be a time of trouble, such as never was since there was a nation even to that same time: and at that time thy people shall be delivered, every one that shall be found written in the book   Daniel 12:1

The phrase *stand up* is a poor translation of the original Hebrew: It actually means to "stand aside". This was verified by the apostle Paul.

[5] *Remember ye not, that, when I was yet with you, I told you these things?*
[6] *And now ye know what withholdeth that he might be revealed in his time.*
[7] *For the mystery of iniquity doth already work: only he who now letteth will let, until he be taken out of the way.*
[8] *And then shall that Wicked be revealed, whom the Lord shall consume with the spirit of his mouth, and shall destroy with the brightness of his coming*   II Thessalonians 2:5-8

After Satan and his angels war against Michael and his angels, he will be cast down to earth (Revelation 12:9). This will start the last 3.5 years of the tribulation period and the wrath of Satan. Satan will be allowed to do this by God. The reason was revealed in Daniel 12:1: So that God's chosen people of Israel will finally recognize that Jesus Christ is the Son of God, and that *thy people shall be delivered.*

Jesus referred to Satan as *the prince of this world* (John 12:31), and Paul called him *the prince of the power of the air* (Ephesians 2:2), and *the god of this world* (2 Corinthians 4:4). John also concedes that Satan is a powerful advisary when he says: *We know that we are of God, and the whole world is in the power of the evil one* (1 John 5:19). These references leave us with the question: *In what sense does Satan rule the world*? The Holy Scriptures frequently use the term *the world* or *this world* to refer to the present evil which exists in many forms throughout the entire world. The Bible never teaches that Satan actually rules as a monarch or king over the entire world, but that he is ruler over the current system of sinful opposition to God. In other words, he and his army of fallen angels is constantly trying to oppose everything for which God stands.

Satan and all of his *fallen angels* are spiritual beings and possess no bodies, and we often refer to them as demonic creatures or simply *demons*. There is a great deal of debate among biblical scholars as to the classification of demons. Some hold that demons are not angels, but quite different. This concept should be rejected, because if demons are different from angels then where did they come from? In the beginning before the earth was inhabited, God created millions of angels and they were all pure and good. When Satan rebelled against God and was cast out of heaven, he took 1/3 of all these angels with him (Revelation 12). It is believed that these angels became wicked and evil after they were confined to earth, and sought to inhabit the physical bodies of men and women. They are called *disembodied spirits* who are wicked, unclean, and vicious. They are constantly seeking to enter the body of either a believer or an unbeliever to execute their plan. Some biblical teachers assert that the angelic beings which follow Satan cannot reside in a born-again Christian, but this is a myth. Christians are just as susceptible to demonic influence as any other person. The difference is that each born-again Christian has a power that is greater than Satan within them; called the *Holy Spirit*. It is clear that even priests, pastors and clergy hide demonic control in their lives. Homosexual behavior, adultery, lying and addiction to prostitution have been widely reported and documented. The belief that a Christian cannot be indwelled by demons is simply a Satanic lie from hell. There is a constant war within each Christian between the Holy Spirit and Satanic demons. Of course, it is much easier for demons to win these battles within a non-believer than with a born-again believer.

Can Demons cause disease and sickness?

Many sicknesses and illness are caused by demons attacking our physical bodies. The influence of demons on our health is more severe than might be realized. Many preachers will boldly declare that *all* illness is caused by demons. The logic is that Jesus Christ spent His entire ministry healing the sick, destroying infirmities, restoring sight to the blind and making the lame whole. There was never an incident recorded in which illness of any kind was instigated by Jesus, but demons can and will cause sickness and bodily harm. Jesus Christ working through a born-again Christian with the *gift of healing* can heal anybody of anything…even raise the dead. The principle of choice is at work in this entire scenario. If a person walks around in winter with no shoes or shirt, they are surely asking for a winter cold. Many people bring serious illness upon themselves, and then blame God. My own mother smoked all of her life, and was warned at an early age that she risked getting lung cancer. She continued to smoke heavily and in her 60's she was diagnosed with terminal lung cancer. She was a fine Christian all of her life, and as she lay dying she turned to me and said: *Why is God doing this to me?* I lovingly corrected her and replied; *God did not do this to you, you did it to yourself.* She never complained or blamed God again, and shortly after she passed away. Conversely, many sicknesses are brought about by demons and may or may not be the fault of the person involved. In this case, one must ask the Holy Spirit to recognize the source of the problem, or petition Jesus Christ to intercede no matter what caused the illness or infirmity. In the latter case, there is a specific procedure which has been given to us in the Holy scriptures.

*Is any sick among you? let him call for the **elders** of the church; and let them pray over him, anointing him with oil in the name of the Lord*   James 5:14

A word of caution: If anyone claims to have the Gift of Healing, and the instructions of God are not being followed …stay away from that individual.

An example of the former was when Jesus Christ healed the mother-in-law of Simon.

[38] *And he arose out of the synagogue, and entered into Simon's house. And Simon's wife's mother was taken with a great fever; and they besought him for her*
[39] *And he stood over her, and rebuked the fever; and it left her: and immediately she arose and ministered unto them*   Luke 4:38-39

Note that if this fever was caused by some physical act of Simon's mother-in-law, then why would Christ *rebuke* the fever? That would be pure nonsense. One can only rebuke something that can understand and possess intelligence. In this case, Christ knew that the fever was caused by a demon and commanded it to leave. The fever left the woman because Christ had removed its source. She was immediately healed and began serving Christ.

Satan and his demonic forces are all *spirit beings* that were created by God. As spirit beings, they cannot be treated in the same way as mankind; who are body, soul and spirit. The ultimate fate of demonic spirit beings is to be permanently removed from God's presence. The Bible is not clear on when this will happen. but we do know that after this earth is renovated by fire and the new earth emerges, sin, death and all forms of sickness will be destroyed (Nahum 1:9-10). The host of demons who follow Satan will no doubt be cast into the Lake of Burning Fire where they will be tortured forever with Satan. There are two points in time at which these Demons might be incarcerated forever. The first is following the Battle of Armageddon just before the Millennial Kingdom begins, and the second is after the final battle that God has with Satan at the end of the Millennial Kingdom. Any conclusion of when they might meet their fate would only be speculation.

Chapter 5
The Spirit World

God has existed forever with no beginning and no end. In the ageless past He created angels without sin to serve Him and worship Him. These created beings were called *angels*. Not all angels were created equally. The scriptures tell us that the most powerful, beautiful and exalted angel was called *Lucifer*. Before he led a rebellion against God and was cast out of heaven, Lucifer or *Satan* ruled over all of the angels, several of which are identified and named in the Holy Scriptures.

1. *Archangels*
   - Michael
   - Gabriel
2. *Special Angels*
   - Seraphim
   - Cherubim
3. *Common Angels*
   - Holy angels
   - Rebellious angels
   - Fallen angels
2. *Other Angels*
   - Abaddon/Apollyon
   - The 7 angels of the presence

Lucifer (bright Light)

Lucifer was evidently the most powerful angel that God ever created. Sometime in the dateless past Lucifer wanted to be like God and rebelled against the Most High. We are not told of the great battle that must have ensued, but Lucifer was defeated and he was cast out of heaven (Ezekiel 28:13-15)) with 1/3 of all the common angels that chose to follow him (Revelation 12). Sometime later in time, Lucifer appeared in the Garden of Eden as a beautiful serpent and tempted Adam and Eve by calling God a deceptor and a liar. God had warned Adam and Eve that if they were to eat of the Tree of Good and Evil, they would *surely die*. Lucifer convinced Eve that if she and Adam ate of the Tree of Good and Evil that they would not die, but would be wise and be just like God. From that point on, Lucifer was commonly referred to as *Satan* (enemy or adversary), and his corrupted angels were known as

demons. Demons are spirit beings who roam the world trying to find a body that they can operate out of to deceive all mankind and tempt them to sin. They can also cause sickness, infirmities and even madness in extreme cases (Mark 5:1-20). Christians should constantly be reminded that Satan is their enemy who seeks to maim, kill and destroy (John 10:10). He is a *liar and the father of lies* (John 8:44). Demonic forces are constantly at enmity with Christians and war against them. *For we wrestle not against **flesh** and blood, but against principalities, against powers, against the rulers of the darkness of this world, against spiritual wickedness in high places* (Ephesians 6:12).

Gabriel (God is my strength)

Gabriel is referred to in Luke 1:11 as an *angel of the Lord*. Gabriel is never called an archangel in the Holy Bible, but is identified as one in the ancient Book of Enoch. *Gabriel* is the messenger from God who bring important news to individuals. Daniel the prophet prayed to God for wisdom and understanding, and God sent Gabriel to Daniel (Daniel 8:15–26, 9:21–27). In the Gospel of Luke, Gabriel appeared to Zechariah and the Virgin Mary, foretelling the births of John the Baptist and Jesus (Luke 1 :11-38).

Gabriel by Pinturicchio
(1500 AD)

Michael (who is like God)

Michael is the archangel who was destined to be the great protector of Israel (Daniel 12:1). It is Michael who is constantly at war with Satan on our behalf (Daniel 10:13). In Jude we see Michael confronting Satan concerning the body of Moses (Jude 1:9). Most biblical scholars identify the pre-incarnate Christ as the *angel of light* (Exodus 13:31-32) who led Moses and the people through the wilderness. However, it could have been Michael. Michael is destined to fight against Satan and his angelic forces in the heavenlies. In the book of Revelation, we see that there is a war in heaven. The opposing sides are described as Michael and his angels against the dragon which we know to be Satan and his angels. Satan will be defeated and cast down to earth. It is this conflict which signals the beginning of the wrath of Satan against the earth and the last 3.5 years of the tribulation period.

[7] *And there was war in heaven: Michael and his angels fought against the dragon; and the dragon fought and his angels,*
[8] *And prevailed not; neither was their place found any more in heaven.*
[9] *And the great dragon was cast out, that old serpent, called the Devil, and Satan, which deceiveth the whole world: he was cast out into the earth, and his angels were cast out*

with him.

[10] *And I heard a loud voice saying in heaven, Now is come salvation, and strength, and the kingdom of our God, and the power of his Christ: for the accuser of our brethren is cast down, which accused them before our God day and night.*

[11] *And they overcame him by the blood of the Lamb, and by the word of their testimony; and they loved not their lives unto the death.*

[12] *Therefore rejoice, ye heavens, and ye that dwell in them. Woe to the inhabiters of the earth and of the sea! for the devil is come down unto you, having great wrath, because he knoweth that he hath but a short time.*   Revelation 12:7-12

The Greek word for wrath in Revelation 12:12 is a strong word; *thumas*. There are two words for wrath in the Greek; One is *orge* which means a "quiet, controlled rage"; the other is *thumas* which means an "uncontrollable great rage".

The Seraphim (fiery, burning ones)

The seraphim are angelic beings associated with the prophet Isaiah's vision of God in His Temple, when God called him to his prophetic ministry.

[1] *In the year that king Uzziah died I saw also the Lord sitting upon* a
throne, high and lifted up, and his train filled the temple.

[2] *Above it stood the seraphims: each one had six wings; with twain he covered his face, and with twain he covered his feet, and with twain he did fly.*

[3] *And one cried unto another, and said, Holy, holy, holy, is the LORD of hosts: the whole earth is full of his glory.*   Isaiah 6:1- 3

Seraphim is the plural of *seraph*. The word seraphim appears three times in the Torah (Numbers 21:6–8, Deuteronomy 8:15), and four times in the Book of Isaiah (6:2–6, 14:29, 30:6. In the Book of Revelation (Revelation 4) the seraphim are described as being forever in God's presence and praising him. *Day and night without ceasing they sing: Holy, holy, holy is the Lord God Almighty, who was and is and is to come*   Revelation 4:6-9.

The Cherubim (Guardians)

Cherubim is the plural form of *Cherub*. They are first mentioned in the Bible in Genesis 3.

After He drove the man out, He placed on the east side of the Garden of Eden cherubim and a flaming sword flashing back and forth to guard the way to the tree of life   Genesis 3:24.

It is unfortunate that many people associate a cherub with a cute little baby having wings. The truth is that Cherubs are mighty, fierce creatures who serve as guardians for God. Prior to his rebellion, Satan was a cherub (Ezekiel 28:12-15). The tabernacle and temple along with their articles contained many representations of cherubim (Exodus 25:17-22; 26:1, 31; 36:8; 1 Kings 6:23-35; 7:29-36; 8:6-7; 1 Chronicles 28:18; 2 Chronicles 3:7-14; 2 Chronicles 3:10-13; 5:7-8; Hebrews 9:5). They stood over the Ark of the Covenant spreading their wings.

The prophet Ezekiel had a vision in which he saw Cherubim (Ezekiel 1:1-23) He saw *four living creatures*, each had four faces; like that of a man, a lion, an ox, and an eagle; and each had four wings. In their appearance, the cherubim *had the likeness of a man* (Ezekiel 1:5). These cherubim used two of their wings for flying and the other two for covering their bodies (Ezekiel 1:6,11, 23). Under their wings the cherubim appeared to have the form, or likeness, of a man's hand (Ezekiel 1:8;10:7-8, 21).

The main difference between the types of heavenly beings known as *cherubim and seraphim* is there appearance: *cherubim* have four faces and four wings, while *seraphim* have six wings. Cherubim have 4 faces and Seraphim have only one. In the Bible, the main role of both cherubim and seraphim is to sit by the throne of God and worship Him continually. It also appears that the Cherubim also transport God in a chariot on special occasions (Ezekiel 1&2).

Common Angels

Common Angels were created by God sometime in the dateless past. How many were created we do not know, but in Revelation 5:11 we are told that the number of angels that are now in existence are too large to count. There are *myriads of myriads, and thousands of thousands of angels*. The Greek word for "myriads" can be translated as tens of thousands (10,000). This would mean that there are more than 100 million (100,000,000) angels. *That is a lot of angels!* All of the angels were created holy and to serve God, but some became wicked and suffered the consequences. (1) When Satan was cast out of heaven he took 1/3 of all the angels with him (Revelation 12: 1-4). These angels are now barred from heaven and serve Satan. They are referred to in the Holy Scriptures as *rebellious angels*.(2) Two-thirds of all the angels remained with God and they are called *Holy angels*. (3) After Satan was cast out of heaven with his rebellious angels, there were a few angels called *sons of God* who left and descended upon earth to have sexual relations with *daughters of men*. The "sons of God" almost surely refer to angels (Job 1:6, 2:1, 36:7). Peter wrote that these angels are now being held in prison where they await their final punishment (II Peter 2:4). They were visited by God after His resurrection from the grave.

[18] *For Christ also hath once suffered for sins, the just for the unjust, that he might bring us to God, being put to death in the flesh, but quickened by the Spirit:*
[19] *By which also he went and preached unto the spirits in prison;*
[20] *Which sometime were disobedient, when once the longsuffering of God waited in the days of Noah, while the ark was a preparing, wherein few, that is, eight souls were saved by water.*   I Peter 3:18-20

Intercourse with women resulted in production of offspring who were known as *Nephilim* who were a race of giants (Genesis 6:4). Because of this transgression and the evil character of mankind, God was moved to flood the world with water and destroy every human but Noah, his sons and their wives; 8 in all. As punishment for what they had done, God cast all of the angels who participated into the bottomless pit. They will be removed and cast into the Lake of Burning Fire at the last judgment:

And the angels which kept not their first estate, but left their own habitation, he hath reserved in everlasting chains under darkness unto the judgment of the great day   Job 6

What does it mean that these angels *kept not their first estate*? Understanding this phrase solves a great mystery. It means that these angels assumed the bodies of men to have sexual relations with women. The Book of Hebrews verified that this could happen (Hebrews 13:2). The fallen angels which produced a race of giants by cohabitating with earthly women were also called *watchers*. They are described in the ancient Book of Jubilees.

> **And he (Enoch)testified to the Watchers, who had sinned with the daughters of men; for these had begun to unite themselves, so as to be defiled, with the daughters of men, and Enoch testified against all.**   Jubilees 4:2)

> **And it came to pass when the children of men began to multiply on the face of the earth and daughters were born unto them, that the angels of God saw them on a certain year of this jubilee, that they were beautiful to look upon; and they took themselves wives of all whom they chose, and they bare unto them sons and they were giants**   Jubilees 4:1-2

> **Owing to the fornication wherein the Watchers against the law of their ordinances went a whoring after the daughters of men, and took themselves wives of all which they chose.**   Jubilees 7:21

Finally, there is a common belief that all Christians have a *guardian angel* assigned to them for divine protection. There is no Biblical passage that can sustain this assumption, although Matthew 18:10 suggests that this might be possible. Of course, angels often can and do get involved in the affairs of man. Angels protect humans (Daniel 6:20-23; 2 Kings 6:13-17); They help guide people (Matthew 1:20-21; Acts 8:26); They provide for needs (Genesis 21:17-20; 1 Kings 19:5-7); And they provide information or general assistance (Luke 1:11-20; Acts 7:52-53; Hebrews 1:14). Although there is no biblical support for assigned guardian angels, they do administer to the saints upon the command of God.

[13] *But to which of the angels said he at any time, Sit on my right hand, until I make thine enemies thy footstool?*
[14] *Are they not all ministering spirits, sent forth to minister for them who shall be heirs of salvation?*   Hebrews 1:13-14

Angels are probably more active in the affairs of Christians than we currently can visualize or understand.

Abaddon (Apollyon)

Abaddon is a mighty angel who at some time committed a grievous (unknown) sin against God. As a result, God had him bound in chains and committed to the *Bottomless Pit*. Abaddon is now the King of an army of demonic locusts who will be released along with Abaddon to persecute mankind for 5 months during the Great Tribulation to come.

And they had a king over them, which is the angel of the bottomless pit, whose name in the Hebrew tongue is Abaddon, but in the Greek tongue hath his name Apollyon.
Revelation 9:11

Angels of the Presence

Finally, we should mention that there are 7 angels who continually stand before the throne of God; they are called the 7 *angels of His presence*.

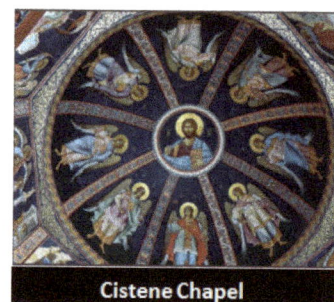

Cistene Chapel

[1] *And when he had opened the seventh seal, there was silence in heaven about the space of half an hour.*
[2] *And I saw the seven angels which stood before God; and to them were given seven trumpets*   Revelation 8:1-2

These angels serve God and will be given a special privilege during the last 3.5 years of the tribulation period. They will each be given a trumpet to sound after the 6th seal is broken on the large scroll (Revelation 5 & 6). As each angel sounds, one of the 7 trumpet judgments will fall upon the earth (Revelation 8-11). The Holy Bible does not give us the name of these angels, but they are named in the ancient Books of Enoch (I Enoch 20:2-8,) and Tobit (Tobit 12:15). Both identify these seven angels as *Uriel, Raphael, Raguel, Michael, Saraqael, Gabriel* and *Remiel.* Gabriel is the archangel preciously discussed:

And the angel answering said unto him, I am Gabriel, that stand in the presence of God
Luke 1:19

Dionysius and Angels (1st Century AD)

According to medieval Christian theologians, the angels are organized into several orders, or *Angelic Choirs*. Dionysius (*On the Celestial Hierarchy*) and Thomas Aquinas (*Summa Theologica*) drew on passages from the New Testament, specifically Ephesians 1:21 and Colossians 1:16, to develop a schema of three Hierarchies of angels called *Spheres*, with each Hierarchy containing three Orders or *Choirs*. Although both authors drew on the New Testament, the Biblical canon is relatively silent on the subject, and these hierarchies are considered less definitive than the biblical material presented in this book.

First Sphere

The first sphere of angels serve as the heavenly servants of God.

- Seraphim
- Cherubim
- Thrones

Second Sphere

The second sphere of angels serve as the heavenly servants of God.

- Dominions
- Virtues
- Powers

Third Sphere

The third sphere of angels serve as the heavenly servants of God.

- Principalities
- Archangels
- Angels

SERAPHIM – sometimes called "the burning ones" because they are closest to God and radiate Pure Light. These are the Angels who constantly sing God's praise, and whose duty it is to regulate the heavens. (Lucifer is said to have been one of the Seraphim who had outshone all the others untill he became the head of the fallen angels).

CHERUBIM – sent to guard the gates of Eden. Originally they were depicted as the bearers of God's Throne, as the charioteers, and as powerful beings with four wings and four faces. However, in modern times, Cheribum have evolved into chubby babies with wings.

THRONES – called the 'many eyed ones' have the duty of carrying out God's decisions. They are often represented as firey wheels.

DOMINIONS – their job is to regulate the duties of the other Angels and ensure that God's wishes are carried out.

VIRTUES – the Angels of Grace who bring God's blessings to Earth, usually in the form of miracles. Known as the 'brilliant' or "shinning'" ones, they are associated with acts of heroism and bring courage when needed.

POWERS – their job is to prevent the 'fallen angels' from taking over the world and keeping the Universe in balance. They are also seen as the Angels of birth and death.

PRINCIPALITIES – the Guardian Angels of cities, nations and rulers, and guards against the invasion of evil angels.

ARCHANGELS – probably the best known of all Angels. They carry God's most important messages to humans. They also command God's 'armies' of Angels in the constant battle with the "sons of darkness."

ANGELS – the Celestial Beings closest to humans. They act as intermediaries between the Almighty and humanity. Often called our "Guardian Angels."

WIKIPEDIA
The Free Encyclopedia

We have spent some time identifying the classification and activities of the angels created by God, their relationship with God, and where they are today. We have mentioned that some are being held in different subterranean compartments until God is ready to either judge them or to use them. We will now discuss the judgment which will fall upon those who are saved, those who are unsaved and those angels now being held in subterranean regions.

Chapter 6

The Resurrections and Judgments of God

The average Christian is aware that there is a time of *Great Tribulation* coming that is described in the *Book of Revelation*; written by the Apostle John around 90 AD. John was caught up into the 3rd heaven and in the spirit he was transported into the future and actually *saw* what he was told to write. There is a great deal of debate as to whether the tribulation period is 7 years long or only 3.5 years in duration. Either viewpoint will agree that during the last 3.5 years of the tribulation period, the *Wrath of Satan* will be unleashed upon all who dwell upon the earth. The Wrath of Satan is the *7 trumpet judgments* which are released by 7 angels at the command of God. The 7 trumpet judgments are immediately followed by the *Wrath of God* which fall upon those who dwell upon the earth. All agree that the Wrath of God will not fall upon those who are saved, and that this wrath is executed through the *7 Bowl Judgments*. It is beyond controversy that the Wrath of God is the 7 bowl judgments (Revelation 15:7, 16:1). Following the 7th bowl judgment, all agree that Jesus Christ will return to earth in His 2nd advent. He will meet Satan and his army somewhere near Jerusalem and completely annialate Satan and his followers at the prophesied *Battle of Armageddon*. This will be followed by the 1000 Year *Millennial Kingdom* during which all those from the Nation of Israel who are still alive and have accepted Jesus Christ as their redeemer and long awaited Messiah will finally inherit the land promised to Abraham and King David. The majority of those chosen to enter into the Land of Promise are the 144,000 Messianic Jews who have been sealed for that very purpose in Revelation 7:1-8. They will live and multiply in the promised land for 1000 years. After the 1000 year Millennial Kingdom is over, every person alive (believer or unbeliever) will be removed from the earth. The earth will then be renovated by fire and restored to an Edenic state. This will end recorded time and eternity will begin. This is a very brief review of end-time events. For a detailed discussion of the tribulation period, see Phillips, *Revelation: Mysteries Revealed*.

This chapter is only concerned with the *Resurrection and Judgments* which will take place between when Satan is defeated at the Battle of Armageddon and the earth is purged by fire. There are four resurrection and judgments which will take place during this period of time.

1.0 The *Resurrection of the righteous dead* and the snatching away of the live believers at an event known as the *rapture*.

2.0 The *Bema Seat Judgment* of all believers

3.0 The *Judgment of the Sheep and Goats* (The Rod Judgment)

4.0 The *Great White Throne Judgment* of all unbelievers and those who lived and died during the1000 year Millennial Kingdom.

The following graphic will frame subsequent discussions.

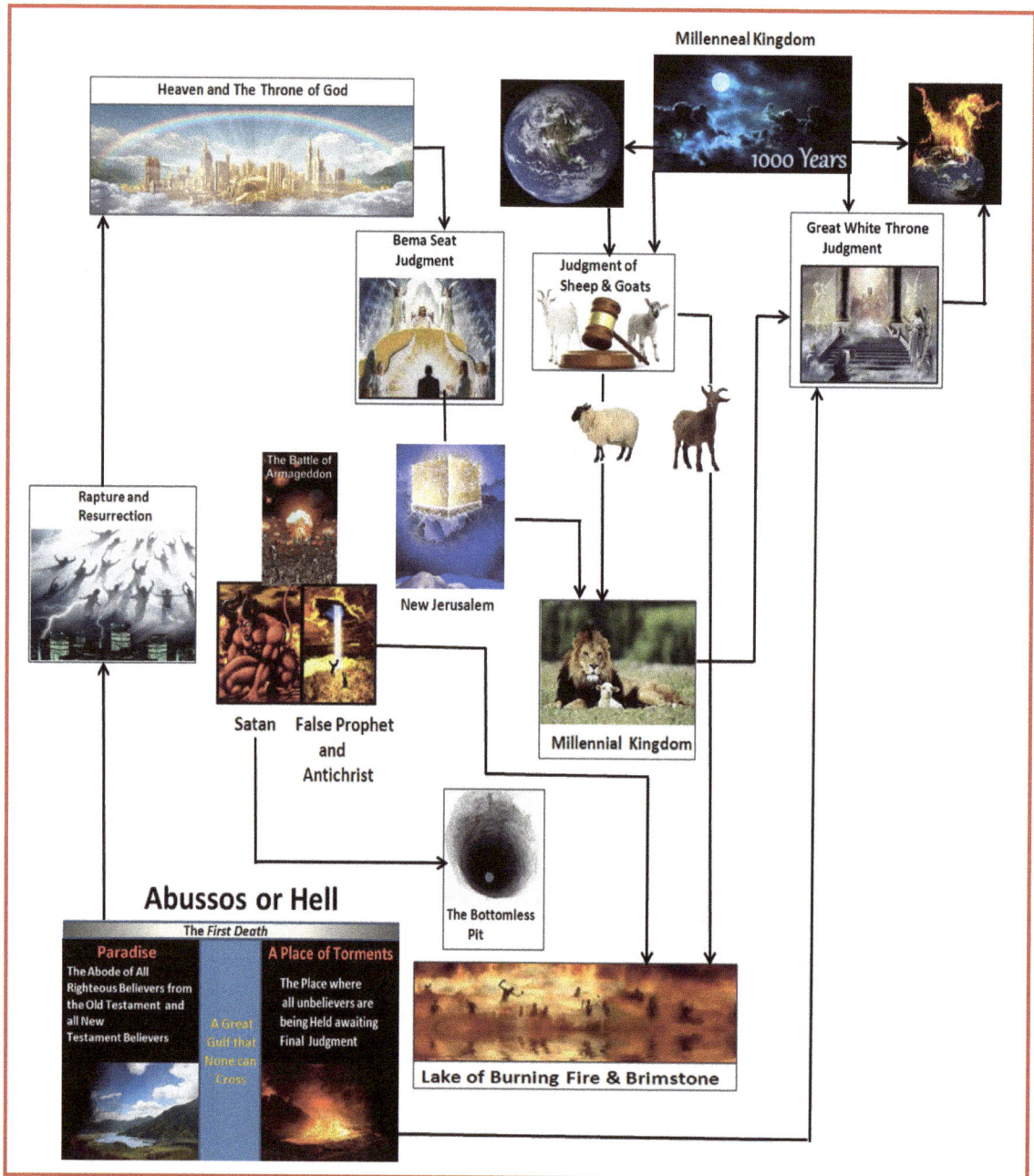

We will also discuss the fate of Satan, the False Prophet and the Antichrist who will persecute all Christians and Jews during the Great Tribulation. It is suggested that the reader carefully study Chapters 3-5 as a precursor to the discussions which follow. The sequence of Resurrections and Judgments which will be discussed are all prophetic and will follow the *Church Age* or the *Dispensation of Grace*, which has been going on since the death of Jesus Christ in 30 AD (Phillips, *The Birth and Death of Jesus Christ;* Phillips, *Dispensations, Covenant Promises and the Eternal Plan of God*).

The *Rapture*

Since the sacrificial death of Jesus Christ in 30 BC almost 2000 years of the *Church Age* or the *Dispensation of Grace* have elapsed. Sometime in the future the Dispensation of Grace will come to an end. This Dispensation will end with a period of time that is called the *Great Tribulation*. Modern scholars all agree that the last 3.5 years of the Church Age will begin when Satan and his rebellious angels engage Michael and the Holy Angels in a great heavenly conflict (Revelation 12:7). The outcome of this battle of good versus evil is that Satan and all of his angels will be cast out of heaven and confined to the earth (Revelation 12:8-9). Satan will be furious, and he will wage war against every Jew and Christian on earth (Revelation 12:17). Many people will join Satan and his forces and be recognized by a sign (666) which will be placed upon their hand or forehead (Revelation 13:7-8, 13-18). The army of Satan will be led by a Satanic-indwelled person called the *Antichrist*, and a religious leader called the *False Prophet* (Revelation 13). The persecution and destruction of earth will be unprecedented in all of previous history. Persecution will last 3.5 years measured as 42 months or 1260 days. Sometime during this period of time, Jesus Christ will suddenly appear in the heavens above earth and call up to Him all who have accepted Him as their Lord and savior; alive or dead. This monumental event is called the *Rapture*. Exactly when the rapture will occur is a hotly debated topic among theologians. Some say it will occur before the Tribulation Period begins (Pre-Trib Rapture); some say that it will occur at the end of the tribulation period (Post-Trib Rapture) and some place it after either the 5th seal is broken (Rosenthal) or after the trumpet judgments (Phillips). Both Rosenthal and Phillips are proponents of a theological position called the Pre-Wrath Rapture. We will not be concerned when it actually occurs, but with what will happen after the Rapture has occurred and after the tribulation period has ended.

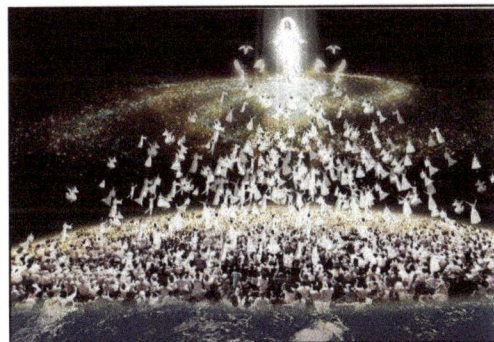

The word "rapture" comes from the Latin *rapere* used in the Latin Vulgate. The **Latin** Bible, or **Vulgate,** was translated from the Hebrew and Aramaic by a scholar known as *Jerome* between 382 and 405 CE. The Greek version of the Bible is called the *Septuagint* (from the Latin word *septuaginta*, which is a translation of the Hebrew Bible into Koine Greek. The Septuagint is also called the *Vulgate*. The vulgate translates the Hebrew as *Harpazo*, which is rendered by the phrase *caught up* in most English translations.

The controversy that exists between those who hold to a Pre-trib, Post-trib or Pre-wrath rapture is not *if* a rapture will occur, but only *when* it will occur. The concept of a rapture of the church is clearly taught in Scripture. The apostle Paul has given us several details of what will happen when the Rapture occurs.

[13] *But I would not have you to be ignorant, brethren, concerning them which are asleep, that ye sorrow not, even as others which have no hope.*

[14] *For if we believe that Jesus died and rose again, even so them also which sleep in Jesus will God bring with him.*

[15] *For this we say unto you by the word of the Lord, that we which are alive and remain unto the coming of the Lord shall not prevent them which are asleep.*

[16] *For the Lord himself shall descend from heaven with a shout, with the voice of the archangel, and with the trump of God: and the dead in Christ shall rise first:*

[17] *Then we which are alive and remain shall be caught up together with them in the clouds, to meet the Lord in the air: and so shall we ever be with the Lord*
I Thessalonians 4:13-17

[51] *Behold, I shew you a mystery; We shall not all sleep, but we shall all be changed,*

[52] *In a moment, in the twinkling of an eye, at the last trump: for the trumpet shall sound, and the dead shall be raised incorruptible, and we shall be changed.*

[53] *For this corruptible must put on incorruption, and this mortal must put on immortality.*

[54] *So when this corruptible shall have put on incorruption, and this mortal shall have put on immortality, then shall be brought to pass the saying that is written, Death is swallowed up in victory*
I Corinthians 15: 51-54

When the *last trumpet* sounds, Christ will suddenly descend from heaven. An Archangel (likely Gabriel) will shout and call forth all of the New Testament saints who died in Christ and those Old Testament men and women of faith who died, believing that a Messiah would arise to redeem them from sin. The dead in Christ will rise first, and then those who are alive will be called up to meet Him in the air (Revelation 11:15-19). The souls of all believers who died in Christ have been waiting in *Paradise*. After they are *resurrected* and called to Christ in the air, all of those on planet earth who are living in faith and have accepted Jesus Christ as their savior will be *caught up* to join Christ in the air. Although debated, scripture seems to be clear of when this will occur.

..and with the trump of God...at the last trump   I Thessalonians 4:16, I Corinthians 15:51

It seems obvious that if there is a *last trump*, it must follow the sounding of *other* trumpets. Is there any place in scripture where this is true?....Yes, at the 7th trumpet in the Book of Revelation.

And the seventh angel sounded; and there were great voices in heaven, saying, The kingdoms of this world are become the kingdoms of our Lord, and of his Christ; and he shall reign forever and ever   Revelation 11:15

It is more than interesting that when the 7th trumpet sounds (the last trumpet) that Christ is about to *take over all of the kingdoms of this world and reign forever*. But if one will continue to read Revelation 11 with an unbiased viewpoint, there is further confirmation.

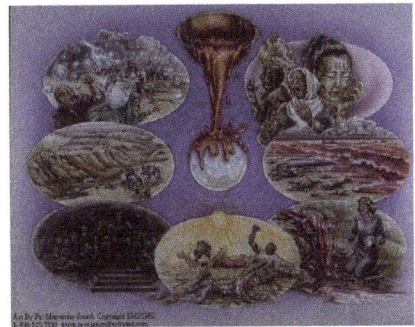

*And the nations were angry, and **thy wrath is come**, and the time of the dead, that **they should be judged**, and that **thou should give reward** unto thy servants the prophets, and **to the saints**, and them that fear thy name, small and great; and should destroy them which destroy the earth*   Revelation 11:18

Note without any preconceived notions what will occur when the 7th trumpet sounds.

(1) The *Wrath of God* has come....This is clearly and unambiguously identified as the 7 Bowl judgments which immediately follow the 7th trump; which is exactly what Revelation 11:18 says will happen following the rapture of the saints. The Wrath of God is described in Revelation 15 &16.

*And one of the four beasts gave unto the seven angels seven golden vials full of the **Wrath of God**, who liveth forever and ever*   Revelation 15:7

*And I heard a great voice out of the temple saying to the seven angels, Go your ways, and pour out the vials of the **Wrath of God** upon the earth*   Revelation 16:1

(2) The time has come or all saints to be judged. This judgment is for *rewards* and not for eternal life

(3) This judgment is for both the prophets (Old Testament) and saints (New Testament).

(4) The time has come for Christ to *put all enemies under his feet*, and to *destroy* those who destroy the earth (Satan, antichrist, False Prophet, demons and followers of Satan)

When do the Holy Scriptures say that these things will take place? At the *Bema seat Judgment* which takes place after the rapture.

The Bema Seat Judgment

The place at which all true believers are rewarded (judged) for their good works is at the *Bema Seat Judgment*. The Bema Seat Judgment will take place before God's throne in heaven, and it will *immediately follow* the sounding of the 7th trump and the rapture or resurrection of all believers. The word Bema is derived from the King James translation in which the Greek word for Bema (bh'ma) is translated as *judgment seat* (John 19:3, Romans 14:10, II Corinthians 5:10).

The apostle Paul speaks clearly on the fact that all righteous men and women will be judged.

For we must all appear before the judgment seat of Christ; that every one may receive the things done in his body, according to that he hath done, whether it be good or bad
II Corinthians 5:10

[10].....*for we shall all stand before the judgment seat of Christ.*
[11] *For it is written, As I live, saith the Lord, every knee shall bow to me, and every tongue shall confess to God.*
[12] *So then every one of us shall give account of himself to God*   Romans 14:10-12

It is interesting that most theologians teach that when we die the soul is immediately transported to God and to his throne. But if rewards and eternal assignments are given immediately following death by God in heaven, then what Paul revealed does not make any sense at all! The key biblical verse used to support that every Christian ascends into heaven and is immediately rewarded with eternal life and assigned duties is II Corinthians 5:6-8 which *immediately* precedes Paul's discussion of the rapture.

[6] *Therefore we are always confident, knowing that, whilst we are at home in the body, we are absent from the Lord:*
[7] *(For we walk by faith, not by sight:)*
[8] **We are confident, I say, and willing rather to be absent from the body, and to be present with the Lord**   II Corinthians 5: 6-8

Paul is *not* saying that at death he will be present with the Lord immediately after death. He is simply saying that he is willing to be absent from the body and be with the Lord. As we have taught, Paul's statements in II Corinthians actually supports that the body separates from the soul and spirit at death and awaits rewards when the resurrection of the righteous dead occurs preceding the rapture of the living. Note that following II Corinthians 5:8 Paul reassures us that rewards will be given only at the *Judgment seat of Christ*; This is the *Bema Seat Judgment* which will follow the Battle of Armageddon. All Pre-tribulation rapture proponents will not address this issue. If there is a pre-tribulation rapture, the entire concept of rewards for service *after* the tribulation period makes no sense at all. There is not a single verse in the New Testament that negates this conclusion. The Pre-Wrath rapture position of either Rosenthal or Phillips is perfectly consistent with this logic.

The Old Testament clearly and repeatedly teaches that the soul *sleeps* awaiting the resurrection from the dead. *Sleep* is used in the Old Testament to describe the state of all men or women after death. Without the existence of any New Testament epistles or of the teachings of Jesus Christ in the 4 gospels; the word *sleep* is simply referring to a state of existence after death. Some teach a concept called *soul sleep*, which is a state of rest after death in which the soul of man enters a state of unconsciousness after death, but soul sleep cannot be justified by the full council of scripture. The Old Testament prophets used the term sleep because they only knew that they would await forgiveness of sins in Paradise in another state of existence.

The Bema Seat Judgment of Christ *does not* determine salvation; that is determined when we accept Jesus Christ as our Lord and Savior (1 John 2:2) and place our faith in Him (John 3:16). All of our sins were forgiven when Christ shed his blood on the Cross of Calvary. The sin issue is finished and sin no longer condemns any New Covenant or Old Testament believer who died in the faith of Abraham (Romans 8:1). The Bema Seat is where rewards are given and positions of servitude and service are given to each believer.

[6] *Even as **Abraham** believed God, and it was accounted to him for righteousness.*
[7] *Know ye therefore that they which are of faith, the same are the children of **Abraham**.*
[8] *And the scripture, foreseeing that God would justify the heathen through faith, preached before the gospel unto **Abraham**, saying, In thee shall all nations be blessed.*
[9] *So then they which be of faith are blessed with faithful **Abraham**.*
[14] *That the blessing of **Abraham** might come on the Gentiles through Jesus Christ; that we might receive the promise of the Spirit through faith.*
[29] *And if ye be Christ's, then are ye **Abraham**'s seed, and heirs according to the promise*
Galatians 3: 6-9, 14, 29

The Five Christian Crowns

The Crown of Righteousness
(2 Timothy 4:8)

The Crown of Life
(James 1:12; Rev. 2:10)

The Crown of Glory
(1 Peter 5:4)

The Incorruptible Crown
(1 Corinthians 9:25)

The Crown of Rejoicing
(1 Thessalonians 2:19)

We should not look at the Judgment Seat of Christ as God judging our sins, but rather as God rewarding us for our works. We are not saved by works, but we will all receive eternal rewards and *crowns* for serving Christ. Not all works are done in the name of the Lord and for the right reasons; some will be cast away.

65

[11] *For other foundation can no man lay than that is laid, which is Jesus Christ.*
[12] *Now if any man build upon this foundation gold, silver, precious stones, wood, hay, stubble;*
[13] *Every man's work shall be made manifest: for the day shall declare it, because it shall be revealed by fire; and the fire shall try every man's work of what sort it is.*
[14] *If any man's work abide which he hath built thereupon, he shall receive a reward.*
[15] *If any man's work shall be burned, he shall suffer loss: but he himself shall be saved; yet so as by fire*   I Corinthians 3:11-15

Galatians 3 and I Corinthians 3 prove that all believers will be granted eternal life by faith and grace, but that not all believers will be equally rewarded in the life to come.

*For we must all appear before the **judgment seat** of Christ; that every one may receive the things done in his body, according to that he hath done, whether it be good or bad*
     II Corinthians 5:10

The imagery is derived from that of Greek games in which a seat would be set high above the finish line of a race, and a judge would sit there to determine who would place, win and show to receive rewards. Thus, the purpose of the Bema Seat of Christ is to examine a Christian's total life. Each will be recompensed for the righteous deeds that have been done. Paul used this analogy in his teachings.

*Wherefore seeing we also are compassed about with so great a cloud of witnesses, let us lay aside every weight, and the sin which doth so easily beset us, and let us run with patience the **race** that is set before us*   Hebrews 12:1

Regardless of when the rapture occurs, the Bema Seat judgment is in heaven *after* the rapture occurs. During the Bema Seat Judgment, the final Wrath of God (7 Bowls) is poured out upon the earth in rapid succession. These are so severe, that mankind could not exist for a very long time. For example, the 5th bowl causes all fresh and saltwater to turn to blood (Revelation 16:3-4).

[3] *And the second angel poured out his vial upon the sea; and it became as the blood of a dead man: and every living soul died in the sea.*
[4] *And the third angel poured out his vial upon the **rivers and fountains of waters**; and they became blood*   Revelation 16:4

It is interesting that every sea creature is said to have a soul. This proves our previous discussion of a soul in Chapter 2. If sea creatures have a soul, then we can safely assert that land creatures do also. However fish, animals and fowl do not possess a soul that lives after death.

The 7 Bowl Judgments are the *Wrath of God* against Satan and all who remain upon the earth after the saints are removed (Revelation 15:7, 16:1; Phillips, *The Book of Revelation: Mysteries*

Revealed). After the 7th Bowl Judgment, the Battle of Armageddon is fought, Satan is chained in the bottomless pit (Revelation 20:1-2). The False Prophet and the Antichrist have already been cast into the *Lake of Burning Fire* (Revelation 19:20-21). The time has come for a little recognized and often ignored judgment: The judgment of the *Sheep and Goats*.

The Sheep and Goat Judgment

The Judgment of the sheep and goats is on the earth and not in heaven. Christ spoke of it in His *Olivet Discourse* during His final night on earth before His crucifixion.

[31] *When the Son of man shall come in his glory, and all the holy angels with him, then shall he sit upon the throne of his glory:*
[32] *And before him shall be gathered all nations: and he shall separate them one from another, as a shepherd divideth his sheep from the goats:*
[33] *And he shall set the sheep on his right hand, but the goats on the left.*
[34] *Then shall the King say unto them on his right hand, Come, ye blessed of my Father, inherit the kingdom prepared for you from the foundation of the world:*
[35] *For I was an hungred, and ye gave me meat: I was thirsty, and ye gave me drink: I was a stranger, and ye took me in:*
[36] *Naked, and ye clothed me: I was sick, and ye visited me: I was in prison, and ye came unto me.*
[37] *Then shall the righteous answer him, saying, Lord, when saw we thee an hungred, and fed thee? or thirsty, and gave thee drink?*
[38] *When saw we thee a stranger, and took thee in? or naked, and clothed thee?*
[39] *Or when saw we thee sick, or in prison, and came unto thee?*
[40] *And the King shall answer and say unto them, Verily I say unto you, Inasmuch as ye have done it unto one of the least of these my brethren, ye have done it unto me.*
[41] *Then shall he say also unto them on the left hand, Depart from me, ye cursed, into everlasting fire, prepared for the devil and his angels:*
[42] *For I was an hungred, and ye gave me no meat: I was thirsty, and ye gave me no drink:*
[43] *I was a stranger, and ye took me not in: naked, and ye clothed me not: sick, and in prison, and ye visited me not.*
[44] *Then shall they also answer him, saying, Lord, when saw we thee an hungred, or athirst, or a stranger, or naked, or sick, or in prison, and did not minister unto thee?*
[45] *Then shall he answer them, saying, Verily I say unto you, Inasmuch as ye did it not to one of the least of these, ye did it not to me.*
[46] *And these shall go away into everlasting punishment: but the righteous into life eternal*
Matthew 25: 31-46

All living believers were *raptured* from the earth after the 7th trumpet sounded. Satan was bound in the bottomless pit; the antichrist and the false prophet were cast into the Lake of Fire; and all of Satan's army at the Battle of Armageddon were destroyed by God and their souls escorted to the *Place of Torments* with all other unbelievers. The people on earth who remain are from every country throughout the world. They are composed of those individuals who have accepted Christ as their Lord and savior during the 7 Bowl Judgments, and individuals who are still alive and have not been saved. The judgment of the sheep and goats is to determine who will be allowed to enter the 1000 year Millennium kingdom with the 144,000 Messianic Jews who were sealed for that purpose in Revelation 7:1-8.

All of the people on earth who remain alive will be brought before Jesus Christ and He will separate them into two groups: The *Sheep* will be sent to His *left* and the *Goats* to His *right*. The sheep will be allowed to enter into the Millennial Kingdom, and the Goats will be sent to everlasting punishment in the Lake of Fire and Brimstone (Matthew 25:41-46). Clearly, all of those who allowed to enter into the Millennial Kingdom must accept Jesus Christ as their Lord and Savior. They and the 144,000 sealed Messianic Jews were not raptured out before the Bowl Judgments, but survive for a particularly important task: to live in the Millennial Kingdom. The criteria for being chosen from the nations to enter into the Millennial Kingdom is not well understood. Many of those chosen to live upon the earth from that time forward will be *surprised* (Matthew 25:37). This is very strange; a true believer would *not* be surprised, they would understand Matthew 24-25 and would be doing what Christ commanded them to do during His 3.5 year ministry. There must be a large group who is living a righteous and holy life, not because Christ has commanded them to do so but because they are full of Christ-like attributes. They may not have even seen a bible or heard of a messiah named Jesus Christ. Such are those in deepest Africa and in the deepest reaches of the Himalayan Mountains. This is an extraordinary confirmation of the grace and love of Jesus Christ.

The surprise expressed is not at their being told that they acted from love to *His brethren*, but that Christ Himself was the *Personal Object* of all their deeds: that they found Him hungry, and supplied Him with food: that they brought water to Him, and quenched His thirst; that seeing Him naked and shivering, they put warm clothing upon Him; paid Him visits when lying in prison for the truth; and sat by His bedside when wracked with sickness. This is the astonishing statement. It shows that Jesus Christ will reward them based upon how they treated *His brethren*. Jesus Christ made the following statement to Saul of Tarsus on the road to Damascus when He suddenly appeared to him in His post-resurrection glory.

Saul, Saul, why persecutest thou me?   Acts 22:7

This is an astounding statement! Jesus Christ accused Saul of persecuting Him, but He had been crucified, buried and resurrected to the Father many days before that encounter!! Never doubt that a Christian has a personal relationship with Jesus Christ. When you suffer, He suffers; when you feel pain, He feels pain; and when you feel persecution He feels persecution.

Jesus will send the *sheep* to His left as a sheppard foals His sheep at evening. Would any true Christian be surprised or astonished? Does not every Christian know that it is the will of Jesus Christ to take care of His sheep?

[7] *Then said Jesus unto them again, Verily, verily, I say unto you, I am the door of the sheep.*
[9] *I am the door: by me if any man enter in, he shall be saved, and shall go in and out, and find pasture.*
[11] *I am the good shepherd: the good shepherd giveth his life for the sheep*
    John 10: 7, 9, 11

It is more believable that many should be *astonished*, and almost doubt their own ears to hear that they were chosen by grace. Their salvation will come from the lips of the Lord Jesus Christ who has come in His glory, and now sits upon the throne of His glory, and all the holy angels are with Him; and that it is from those glorified Lips that the words come forth, ***Ye did all this unto Me***. This type of judgment should not be a surprise to the Christian who has studied and understood the Old Testament between Adam and the giving of the Law at Mt. Sinai. All of these brethren were judged in the same way: Some went to Paradise and others to a Place of Torments.

The *Sheep and Goat Judgment* was revealed to all of His disciples during His last night on earth on the Mount of Olives. The Dispensation of the Law was coming to a close. In less than 24 hours, Jesus Christ would die on the Cross of Calvary. The judgment of the Sheep and Goats which immediately precedes the 1000 year Millennial Kingdom is also sometimes called the *Judgment of the Nations* (Matthew 25:32). It is not generally recognized, but the Sheep and Goat judgment was prophesied to the Jews by Ezekiel long before Christ spoke of it.

[33] *As I live, saith the Lord GOD, surely with a mighty hand, and with a stretched out arm, and with fury poured out, will I rule over you:*
[34] *And I will bring you out from the people, and will gather you out of the countries wherein ye are scattered, with a mighty hand, and with a stretched out arm, and with fury poured out.*
[35] *And I will bring you into the wilderness of the people, and there will I plead with you face to face.*
[36] *Like as I pleaded with your fathers in the wilderness of the land of Egypt, so will I plead with you, saith the Lord GOD.*
[37] *And I will cause you to pass under the rod, and I will bring you into the bond of the covenant:*
[38] *And I will purge out from among you the rebels, and them that transgress against me: I will*

bring them forth out of the country where they sojourn, and they shall not enter into the
land of Israel: and ye shall know that I am the LORD   Ezekiel 20: 33-38.

Ezekiel prophesied over Israel during the 70 years of Babylonian captivity. In Ezekiel 20, God is revealing to him that a day would come in which Israel would be restored to its land and God would rule over them. ***At that time***, **God** will miraculously gather them out of many countries. The land that they will settle into is the *Land of Israel*. The enemies of Israel (the *rebels*) will not be allowed to enter into the land of Israel (Ezekiel 20:38). There is widespread confusion among prophecy teachers concerning the prophesied return of Israel to the Land of Canaan. Many boldly proclaim that this has begun and started when Israel was recognized as a nation in May of 1948. Since that time, there *has* been a steady migration of Jews from other nations back to Israel;. but this is *not* the return prophesied in Ezekiel 20. The return of Jews to Israel spoken of in this passage of scripture will not occur until *God calls them forth Himself* (Ezekiel 20:34). No *rebels will co-habitate* the land (Ezekiel 20:38). The purpose of this re-gathering is clearly stated: The lord will cause each person to pass beneath His *rod* of judgment. It should be clear that this prophecy is identical to the Judgment of the Sheep and Goat nations in Matthew 25 by Jesus Christ. Of course, the term *nations* is metaphorically speaking of *individuals*, not a land mass.

The earth will be purged of all unbelievers and wicked people who remain alive after the tribulation period has ended in the *Rod Judgment* or equivalently the *Sheep and Goats Judgment*. The 1000 year Millennial Kingdom will begin and peace will reign upon the earth as the Kingdom begins. As incredible as it may seem, even as Jesus Christ and His Bride of Christ will directly rule and reign over all the earth; rebellion, sin and wickedness will arise. This again should be no surprise to those Christians who have studied the Old Testament. The Exodus from Egypt led the nation of Israel out of Egyptian bondage, and then in one of the greatest miracles in the Bible the Red Sea was crossed and God destroyed the Pharaoh and all his army in the sight of every Israelite (Exodus 14:13-31). Approximately 30 days after that miracle, Moses went up on Mt. Sinai to receive the law from God. Upon returning, he found that all of the people had made a *golden idol* to worship, and were engaged in sinful, adulterous activities (Exodus 32). This all happened within the 40 days that Moses was up on Mt. Sinai: Imagine what can happen in 1000 years.

Reward of the Martyrs

In Revelation 19, we are told that at the 2[cd] advent of Christ He fight Satan and his evil forces at the Battle of Armageddon. The result is the total destruction of Satan and his army. As we have previously noted, the Antichrist and the False Prophet will be cast into the Lake of Burning Fire (Revelation 19:20). Satan is taken to Abussos (Bottomless Pit) where he is *shut up* and a mysterious *seal* is placed upon him (Revelation 20:1-3). The next few verses of Revelation 20 are very difficult to interpret with any certainty.

[4] *And I saw thrones, and they sat upon them, and judgment was given unto them: and I saw the souls of them that were beheaded for the witness of Jesus, and for the word of God, and which had not worshipped the beast, neither his image, neither had received his mark upon their foreheads, or in their hands; and they lived and reigned with Christ a thousand years.*

[5] *But the rest of the dead lived not again until the thousand years were finished. This is the first resurrection.*

[6] *Blessed and holy is he that hath part in the first resurrection: on such the second death hath no power, but they shall be priests of God and of Christ, and shall reign with him a thousand years*   Revelation 20:4-6

It is clear that the Apostle John actually *sees* thrones with someone upon each of them; Whoever sits upon these thrones, they are given the power to *judge* those standing before them. Here the narrative breaks (with a colon), so we must pause also. *Who are sitting on the thrones* ? We are given no answer and we must look elsewhere in the Holy Scriptures.

In Matthew 19:28 Christ was speaking to His disciples and revealed that they would one day judge other people.

[27] *Then answered Peter and said unto him, Behold, we have forsaken all, and followed thee; what shall we have therefore?*

[28] *And Jesus said unto them, Verily I say unto you, That ye which have followed me, in the regeneration when the Son of man shall sit in the throne of his glory, ye also shall sit upon twelve thrones, judging the twelve tribes of Israel*   Matthew 19:27-28

It appears that the judgment of Revelation 20 might be a fulfillment of these promises. If the apostles are seen by John in Revelation 20, it would be natural that John would not wonder or ask who these judges were because he would know each of them. This is the best we can do without any further clues *Who is being judged?* As the narrative continues, there is no doubt as to who is being judged: They are *martyrs* who had been killed by the sword.

[7] *And it* (the beast) *was given unto him to make war with the saints, and to overcome them: and power was given him over all kindreds, and tongues, and nations.*

[8] *And all that dwell upon the earth shall worship him, whose names are not written in the book of life of the Lamb slain from the foundation of the world.*

[9] *If any man have an ear, let him hear.*

[10] *He that leadeth into captivity shall go into captivity:* **he that killeth with the sword** *must be killed with the sword. Here is the patience and the faith of the saints*
          Revelation 13:7-10

This group being judged seems to *not* include martyrs from the Church Age, but only those who had died for not denying Christ during the Tribulation Period. Speculation becomes near

71

certainty since they are identified as those who had not worshipped the Beast (Antichrist) and had not taken his mark of "666" (Revelation 20:4).

To complete the interpretation, have we seen the group of martyrs before?...*Yes.*

And when he had opened the fifth seal, I saw under the altar the souls of them that were slain for the word of God, and for the testimony which they held   *Revelation 6:9*

These are martyrs who have refused to deny Jesus Christ are primarily but not necessarily limited to those slain during the Tribulation Period. All were slain for holding fast to the word of God and not denying Jesus Christ. They are in a very special place; They are seen *under the Throne of God* in heaven. They want to be vindicated and ask *How long will God wait to do so?*

[10] *And they cried with a loud voice, saying,* **How long**, *O Lord, holy and true, dost thou not*
    judge and avenge our blood on them that dwell on the earth?
[11] *And white robes were given unto every one of them; and it was said unto them, that **they**
    should rest yet for a little season, until their fellow servants also and their brethren, that
    should be killed as they were, should be fulfilled*   Revelation 6:10-11

That *little season* is until the tribulation Period has run its course.

Armed with spiritual truth, we can nor conjecture what is being seen by John in Revelation 20:4-5. Those who are sitting on thrones and judging are likely the apostles chosen by God to do so through their faith in His Son. All of the apostles had been martyred except John, and are worthy to judge those who have also been martyred and stand before them . This is another judgment for rewards, not condemnation: *they lived and reigned with Christ a thousand years* (Revelation 20:4).

This is the last in a series of judgment which precedes the 1000 year Millennial Kingdom All of these constitute the end of the *1ˢᵗ Resurrection* (Revelation 20:5).

Blessed and holy is he that hath part in the first resurrection: on such the second death hath no power, but they shall be priests of God and of Christ, and shall reign with him a thousand years
    Revelation 20:6

What is this *second death* that is mentioned in Revelation 20:6 ? After another 1000 years is completed, the earth must be purged once again of all wicked and sinful people, just as it was when God sent a great flood which destroyed every man, woman and child except 8 righteous people (Genesis 7:6-7). So, Satan is released from the Bottomless Pit to start another insurrection against God and Jesus Christ. He gathers all the wicked and sinful people to himself, and then gathers them all (again !) outside of Jerusalem. Just as before, Christ appears and completely destroys Satan and all of his followers (Revelation 20:7-9). Satan is cast into the Lake of Burning Fire to be tormented forever (Revelation 20:10). It is now time to judge all of the people who survived the Millennial Kingdom, and all *unbelievers* alive or dead. The time has come for the final, *Great White Throne Judgment*. Those unbelievers who will be judged at The Great White Throne will be condemned to everlasting punishment. This is called the *Second Death*.

The Great White Throne Judgment

The Millennial Kingdom will come to a close with the last great battle between Satan and Jesus Christ.

[7] *And when the thousand years are expired, Satan shall be loosed out of his prison,*

[8] *And shall go out to deceive the nations which are in the four quarters of the earth, Gog and Magog, to gather them together to battle: the number of whom is as the sand of the sea.*

[9] *And they went up on the breadth of the earth, and compassed the camp of the saints about, and the beloved city: and fire came down from God out of heaven, and devoured them.*

[10] *And the devil that deceived them was cast into the lake of fire and brimstone, where the beast and the false prophet are, and shall be tormented day and night forever and ever.*

[11] ***And I saw a great white throne***, *and him that sat on it, from whose face the earth and the heaven fled away; and there was found no place for them.*

[12] *And I saw the dead, small and great, stand before God; and the books were opened: and another book was opened, which is the book of life:* ***and the dead were judged*** *out of those things which were written in the books, according to their works.*

[13] *And the sea gave up the dead which were in it; and death and hell delivered up the dead which were in them: and they were judged every man according to their works.*

[14] *And death and hell were cast into the lake of fire.* ***This is the second death.***

[15] ***And whosoever was not found written in the book of life was cast into the lake of fire***
Revelation 20:7-15

Most Biblical Scholars state that the Great White Throne Judgment is a judgment of only unbelievers, but this cannot be true because it is the last final judgment upon mankind. The Millennial Kingdom began as a pure and sinless place, but the inhabitants had children who turned away from Jesus Christ and Jehovah God. We know that those born during the next 1000 years settled all over the known world, but many failed to honor God. Following the Battle of Armageddon and the Bema Seat Judgment:

[16] *And* ***it shall come to pass, that every one that is left*** *of all the nations which came against Jerusalem shall even go up from year to year to worship the King, the LORD of hosts, and to keep the Feast of tabernacles.*

[17] *And it shall be, that whoso will not come up of all the families of the earth unto Jerusalem to worship the King, the LORD of hosts, even upon them shall be no rain.*

[18] *And if the family of Egypt go not up, and come not, that have no rain; there shall be the*

plague, wherewith the LORD will smite the heathen that come not up to keep the Feast of tabernacles.

[19] This shall be the punishment of Egypt, and the punishment of all nations that come not up to keep the Feast of tabernacles   Zachariah 14:16-19

God will require all of the people to come to Jerusalem once a year to celebrate the *Feast of Tabernacles*, but some will refuse to come. If persons do not come to the Feast of Tabernacles, the Lord will punish that nation or persons by withholding rain. There is a rebellion prophesied for Egypt in particular.

The Great White Throne Judgment will deal with 4 classes of people.

(1) Unbelievers who have died from both the Old and New Testament dispensations or Ages, and those that died during the 1000 year Millennial Kingdom

(2) Unbelievers who will still be alive *in the nations* that have not been gathered to Satan for the last great battle outside of Jerusalem

(3) Those who have accepted Christ and died during the 1000 year Millennial Kingdom

(4) Those who have accepted Christ as their Lord and Savior and remain alive.

The vast majority of those who will be judged will be those who have died without accepting Jesus Christ as their savior. *Every man will be judged according to their works.* Those in Christ will be judged for eternal rewards; those who died without accepting Jesus Christ as their Lord and Savior will be condemned, and the verdict justified by recounting the things that they did and did not do. It is interesting that Revelation 20:12 says that the Lamb's Book of Life was opened and that there were *other books opened.* Although not specifically stated, in the context of Revelation 20:7-15 it can be inferred that there are books which are being kept in heaven by angels which record everything done in life by each individual…. good or bad deeds. This is a frightening thought, but this is not what eventually determines the fate of anyone who has died in faith. Those who refuse the free gift of eternal life by believing in the Son of God will receive the true and just sentencing deserved of them.

And whosoever was not found written in the book of life was cast into the lake of fire
          Revelation 20:15

There is a saying by some wise sage:

Those who are born-again and accept Jesus Christ as their Lord and Savior will only die once. Those who choose to reject salvation and refuse the gift of eternal life by Grace from Jesus Christ will die twice

Chapter 7
Summary and Truth

There are three judgments and one resurrection which will take place at or near the end of the Church Age (Dispensation of Grace).

- The *Resurrection* of the righteous dead and the snatching away of the live believers at an event known as the *rapture*.
- The *Bema Seat Judgment* of all believers
- The *Judgment of* the *Sheep and Goats* (The Rod Judgment)
- The *Judgment for Rewards* of Martyred Saints
- The final Judgment is the *Great White Throne Judgment*
  The resurrection and judgment of all unbelievers, and all of those who died and those that remain alive after the 1000 year Millennial Kingdom.

The Great White Throne Judgment will be the last event before the world is renovated and purged by fire, immediately preceding eternity in a sin-free world.

- ## The Resurrection of the Righteous Dead and the Snatching Away of the Live Believers: The *Rapture*.

The Rapture will occur at the sounding of the 7th Trump. Christ will suddenly and without warning descend from heaven and stop in mid-air above the earth. (1) All of those who died in faith from the Old Testament (Hebrews 11), and all of those from the New Testament who died after accepting Jesus Christ as their Lord and Savior will be resurrected to meet Jesus Christ in the air (2) Those who are still alive after the Wrath of Satan (Revelation 12:17) has fallen upon the earth-dwellers will be translated to meet Jesus Christ in the air (I Thessalonians 4:13-17, I Corinthians 15: 54-57). All will then receive their incorruptible, eternal heavenly bodies. This large group of believers will then follow Christ back to heaven for the Bema Seat Judgment.

- ## The Bema Seat Judgment of all Believers

Christ has gathered to Him all of those who have believed upon Him (John 3:16). The time has come for the faithful to receive the rewards which are laid up for them in heaven at the *Bema Seat Judgment*.

*Rejoice, and be exceeding glad: for great is your **reward** in heaven:.*   Matthew 5:12

*For the Son of man shall come in the glory of his Father with his angels; and then he shall **reward** every man according to his works*
Mathew 16:27

The Bema Seat Judgment is in heaven and will be a judgment for rewards, not a judgment for eternal life. Each of those at the Bema Seat Judgment will be given *Robes of White* and a *new name.*

> [9] *After this I beheld, and, lo, a great multitude, which no man could number, of all nations, and kindreds, and people, and tongues, stood before the throne, and before the Lamb,* **clothed with white robes***, and palms in their hands;*
>
> [13] *And one of the elders answered, saying unto me, What are these which are arrayed in white* **robe***s? and whence came they?*
>
> [14] *And I said unto him, Sir, thou knowest. And he said to me, These are they which came out of great tribulation, and have washed their* **robe***s, and made them white n the blood of the Lamb.*   Revelation 7:9, 13-14

Dressed in Robes of white, all of this group will now follow Christ to the *Wedding Ceremony of the Lamb*, where the Wedding of the Lamb to His Bride will take place (Revelation 19:7-9) . These believers will escape the Wrath of God which is being poured out upon Satan and everyone left upon the earth (Revelation 16:1). All of the New Testament Saints will be the *Bride of Christ*. All of the Old Testament Saints are already married to God, and they will be the *Wedding Guests.*

Turn, O backsliding children, saith the LORD; for **I am married unto you***: and I will take you one of a city, and two of a family, and I will bring you to Zion*   Jeremiah 3:14

What a glorious ceremony it will be! Part of our rewards will be straight from God in the presence of Jesus Christ.

To him that overcometh will I give to eat of the hidden manna, and will give him a white stone, and in the stone **a new name** *written, which no man knoweth saving he that receiveth it*
        Revelation 2:17

Glory of Glories! Each saint will be given the *hidden manna* to eat, and a *new name* written on a *white stone*. This is the ultimate fulfillment of the High Priest seeking truth from God in the Old Testament under the Law of Moses. Recall that the High Priest wore a white garment with the *urim* and the *thummin* in a pouch over his heart. One was a stone of *white* and one a stone of *black*. The high priest would ask God to make a decision by reaching into the pouch and withdrawing one stone. The white stone was *yes* to the question posed to God and the black stone was *white*. God says *yes* to us! Isn't it marvelous to see God and His omnipotence revealed in the Old Testament!!

- ## The Sheep and Goat Judgment (The Rod Judgment)

The Tribulation Period has ended. All believers living and dead have been *raptured* and rewarded at the Bema Seat Judgment. Following the Wrath of God upon the earth (The 7 Bowl Judgments), the Battle of Armageddon has been fought and Satan has been bound with chains and cast into Gehenna (the Bottomless Pit). The Antichrist and the False Prophet have both been thrown into the Lake of Burning Fire. All of those unbelievers who followed Satan to Armageddon have been placed in the Place of Torments to await the Great White Throne Judgment.

The only people who now remain upon earth are the 144,000 Jews who have been sealed so that they can enter into the Land of Canaan and live in the Land promised to Abraham and King David for 1000 years, and the people living in the nations of the world who had not been ither raptured out or called to the Battle of Armageddon. These people are called the *Sheep* and the *Goat* nations. Jesus Christ will summon all of these people to Jerusalem where He will have each person pass under His *Rod of Judgment*. The people of the nations will be separated into two groups: the *Sheep* and the *Goats*. The sheep will be gathered on His right, and the goats on His left. The criteria for separation will be how each individual treated His *brethren*. The sheep will inherit eternal life, and the goats will be cast into the Lake of Burning fire. The Rod Judgment will clear the earth of all unbelievers. The 144,000 sealed Jews and the Sheep nations will inherit the Millennial Kingdom.

- ## Rewards for the Martyrs

Our Lord Jesus Christ offered His own life for the sins of the world when He died upon the Cross of Calvary. Throughout the ages there have been others who have paid the ultimate price for their Lord and Savior. They had not denied Christ and had been martyred for their faith. Many will be beheaded during the Tribulation Period by the Antichrist and his followers. There is a special place in heaven reserved for those faithful believers, and it is beneath the *Throne of God*. They are seen in Revelation 6 pleading with God to *avenge their blood*. These had paid the ultimate price for their faith, and are evidently not sent to Paradise to await their reward but to a place of great honor next to the Throne Room. Jesus Christ will finally reward them just before the Millennial Kingdom begins. In Revelation 24 they are gathered to the side of Jesus and they ruled and reigned with Him for 1000 years. What a wonderful reward it will be!

- ## The Great White Throne Judgment

The Great White Throne Judgment will bring to a close the long centuries of recorded time which are yet to be determined. Since Jesus Christ died on the Cross of Calvary, there have only been two classes of people in the whole world: those individuals who have *accepted Jesus Christ as their Lord and Savior, and those who have rejected Jesus Christ as their Lord and Savior*:

Jews and Gentiles alike. For all New Testament saints who compose the Body of Christ, there is a promise of eternal life in a state of joy, peace and happiness. They will be joined by all the Old Testament Saints who died in faith looking to the glorious appearance of their Messiah who would offer the same to them. These two groups will be joined by those who will accept Jesus Christ as their Lord and savior during the Millennial Kingdom. All other people who ever lived will be judged and found wanting; they will be cast away forever and tormented in the Burning Lake of Fire where they will join Satan, the Antichrist, the False Prophet and all of the fallen and rebellious angels who chose Satan over Jesus Christ. The Lake of Burning Fire is the final destination of unbelievers from all ages. We are actually not told the fate of all of the fallen and rebellious demons who chose to follow Satan and not God, but they are not flesh and blood because they are spirit beings. It is believed that angels cannot die: they will be confined to the Lake of Burning fire with Satan and all unbelievers where they will be tortured forever (Matthew 25:46, Revelation 20:11-15).

God does not choose on His own to condemn anyone to an eternity of punishment in the Lake of Burning Fire, nor does He want to send anyone into eternal punishment. His desire is that everyone be saved, and He pleads with people to come to Him through His son Jesus Christ.

*The Lord is not slack concerning his promise, as some men count slackness; but is **longsuffering** to us-ward, not willing that any should perish, but that all should come to repentance*   II Peter 3:9

Make no mistake about it, eternal salvation does not depend upon one's works or how good they were in this life, but whether or not they believe upon Jesus Christ as their Lord and Savior. On the Cross of Calvary, Christ offered Himself up once and for all for the sins of every individual who would ever live. He took the sins of the entire world upon Himself. He who had no sin became sin for us.

*For He hath made Him to be **sin** for us, who knew no **sin**; that we might be made the righteousness of God in him*   II Corinthians 5:21

 Salvation is not based upon anything but *faith*….and *Abraham believed God and he was declared righteous by his faith*…. it is pure and simple as that. So simple, in fact, that a child can understand how to gain eternal life. But, if we reject Christ's sacrificial death for our sins, then God has no choice but to give us what we deserve. God will not send us to the Lake of Burning Fire forever: *we will send ourselves*. Our eternal destiny thus lies in our own hands. It is a matter of our free will and choice of where we shall spend eternity.

Our Lord Jesus Christ is the *truth*, the *way* and eternal *life* (John 4:6): In order to receive forgiveness there is only *one* way, we need to place our faith and trust in Jesus Christ the only Son of God as our Savior and the Lord of our lives. If we reject the Son of God and salvation by grace, then we reject God's mercy and we condemn ourselves. When we choose that path, we only deserve His righteous condemnation. If we reject Jesus' offer of forgiveness, then there is simply is *no one else* to pay the penalty for your sin except yourself.

There can be no doubt that these conclusions are true. One cannot be a Christian and not believe in the Word of God. One cannot pick and choose which parts of the bible are true and which are not true. The inspired prophets who wrote the Holy Bible did so under the influence of the Holy Spirit. They repeatedly stated that they were transmitting the very Word of God, infallible and authoritative in the highest degree. This is an amazing thing for any writer to say, and if the forty or so men who wrote the Scriptures were wrong in these claims, then they must have been lying, or insane, or both. Jesus said to His disciples:

[1] *Let not your heart be troubled: ye believe in God, believe also in me.*
[2] *In my Father's house are many mansions: if it were not so, I would have told you. I go to prepare a place for you.*
[3] *And if I go and prepare a place for you, I will come again, and receive you unto myself; that where I am, there ye may be also.*
[4] *And whither I go ye know, and the way ye know.*
[5] *Thomas saith unto him, Lord, we know not whither thou goest; and how can we know the way?*
[6] *Jesus saith unto him, I am the way, the truth, and the life: no man cometh unto the Father, but by me*   John 14:1-6

Timothy said: **All Scripture is God-breathed** *and is useful for teaching, rebuking, correcting and training in righteousness, so that the man of God may be thoroughly equipped for every good work*   2 Timothy 3:15-17

"Somebody ought to tell the truth about the Bible. The preachers dare not; they would be driven from their pulpits. Professors in seminary dare not; because they would lose their job. Politicians dare not; they would be ridiculed and defeated. Editors dare not; they would lose subscribers; merchants dare not, because they might lose customers. Men of fashion dare not; fearing that they would lose market share. Even clerks dare not; because they might be discharged. And so I thought I would do it myself".

Col. Robert G. Ingersoll, *The Works of Robert Ingersoll* (1833-1899)

The purpose of this book has been to do just that.

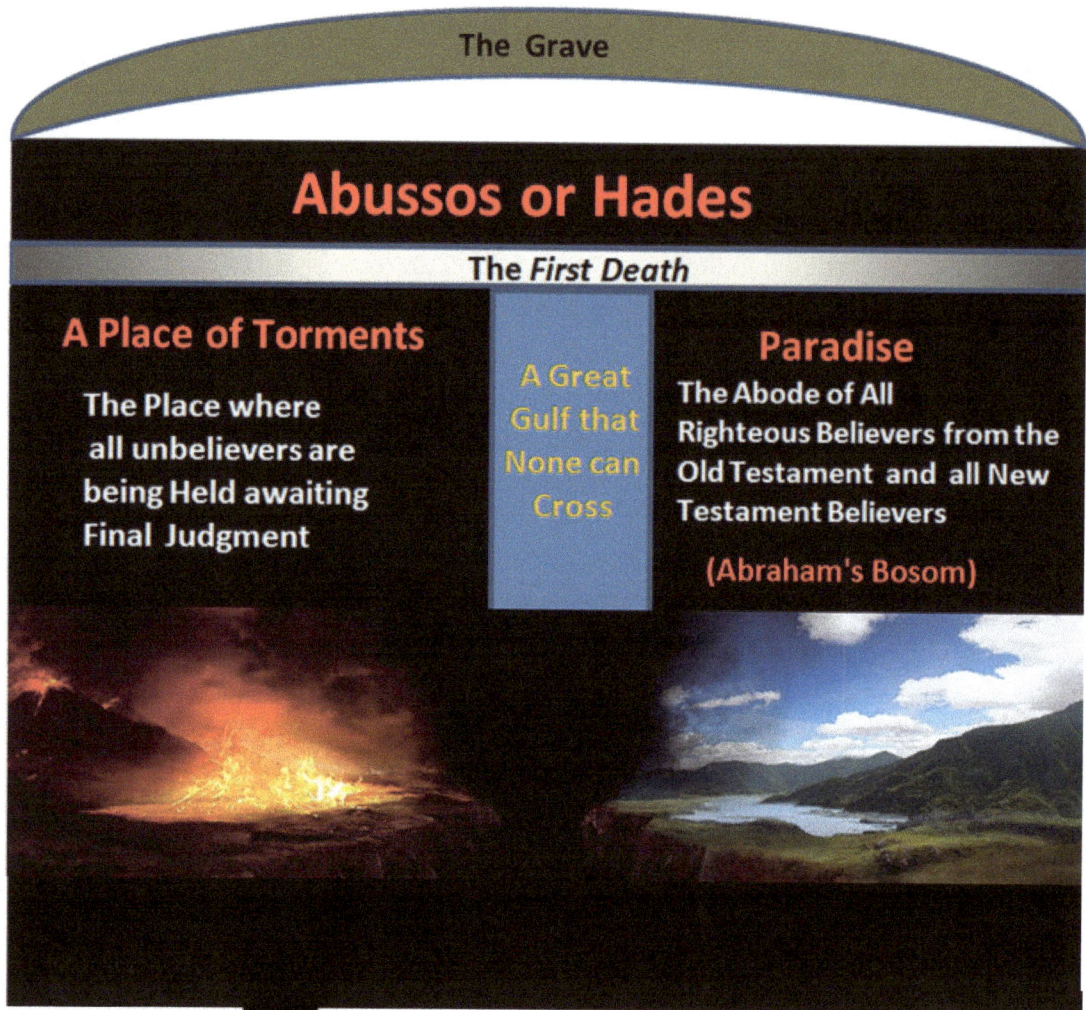

Abussos or Hades

The *First Death*

A Place of Torments

The Place where all unbelievers are being Held awaiting Final Judgment

A Great Gulf that None can Cross

Paradise

The Abode of All Righteous Believers from the Old Testament and all New Testament Believers

(Abraham's Bosom)

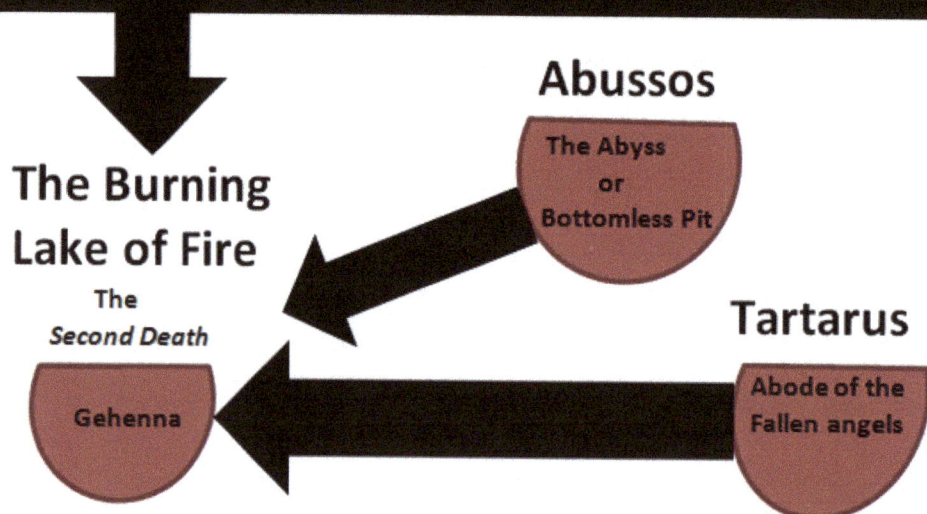

The Burning Lake of Fire

The *Second Death*

Gehenna

Abussos

The Abyss or Bottomless Pit

Tartarus

Abode of the Fallen angels

Bibliography

Larkin, Clarence: *The Greatest Book on Dispensational Truth in the World*, 1918

Toon, Peter*: Heaven and Hell*, 1986

Calvin, John: *Institutes of The Christian Religion*, Vol. 2

W.F. Arndt and F.W. Gingrich*: Greek-English Lexicon of the New Testament*, 1957

Other Books by Don T. Phillips

The Book of Revelation: *Mysteries Revealed*

The Book of Exodus: *Historical and Prophetic Truths*

The Birth and Death of Christ

A Biblical Chronology from Adam to Christ

A Sequential Chronology of End Time Events

A Sequential Chronology of End Time Events: *Expanded Edition*

The Book of Ruth: *Historical and Prophetic Truths*

Dispensations, Covenants and The Eternal Plan of God

All are available from:

Virtualbookworm Publishing Company, PO Box 9949, College Station Texas, 77842
www.virtualbookworm.com

Epilog

This book has attempted to fully explain what happens to a person when they die. It has also discussed the compartments of incarceration that have been reserved for fallen and rebellious angels who left heaven to join Satan and his campaign to overthrow God. The spectrum of resurrections and judgments which will take place after the Church Age has come to a close have also been discussed. In attempting to unravel these eternal mysteries, It is possible that some judgmental interpretation of scriptural truth may have been in error, but I cannot find such a case. I can only hope that this book has caused someone to understand that there is only one Biblical Truth that is absolutely correct: Our Lord Jesus Christ said that **I am the way, the truth and the Life….no man cometh unto the father except by me.** Life on this earth is but a mere spot on the line of time, and the real question is: **where will you spend eternity?** This is the most important question that can ever be asked. The choice is clear: Either in heaven or in the Burning Lake of Fire. Where one will spend eternity depends upon only one thing….*Have you in faith asked Jesus Christ to be your Lord and Savior*? If not, then your soul is destined to face eternal condemnation in the Burning Lake of Fire. Salvation is by faith and not by works…It is offered freely by Jesus Christ. The only requirement is to place your faith in Him. Every person who will ever live will either be granted eternal life in Heaven with our Lord Jesus Christ, or will suffer eternal damnation in the Burning Lake of Fire. The choice is yours. If you want to receive the free gift of eternal life, I ask you to recite the following prayer and believe in its eternal promises

Heavenly Father,
I come to You in prayer asking for the forgiveness of my sins. I confess with my mouth and believe in my heart that Jesus is your Son, and that He died on a Cross at Calvary, that I might be forgiven and have eternal life in the kingdom of Heaven.

Father, I believe that Jesus rose from the dead and I ask you right now to come into my life and be my personal Lord and Saviour. I repent of my sins and will worship You all the days of my life! Because Your word is truth, I confess with my mouth that I am born again and cleansed by the blood of Jesus Christ. In Jesus name I pray, amen.

Friend, If You read this prayer and asked Jesus Christ to be your Lord and Savior, I believe that you will be saved. Find a good bible-based church, and seek the Lord with all your mind and all your heart.

www.ingramcontent.com/pod-product-compliance
Lightning Source LLC
Chambersburg PA
CBHW060946100426
42813CB00016B/2883